the **advanced shotokan** KARATE BIBLE

Acknowledgments

I would like to thank Nita Martin, without whom this book would not have been possible. I would also like to thank Tom Davidson and Andrew Kuc for taking part in the photoshoot.

ASHLEY P. MARTIN

the **advanced shotokan**
KARATE BIBLE
BLACK BELT AND BEYOND

A FIREFLY BOOK

Published by Firefly Books Ltd. 2008

First printing

Publisher Cataloging-in-Publication Data (U.S.)

Martin, Ashley P.
   Advanced shotokan karate : black belt and beyond / Ashley P. Martin.
[208] p. : col. photos. ; cm.
Includes bibliographical references and index.
Summary: A guide for the advanced karate student, providing information needed to progress from a first- to second-degree black belt. It includes step-by-step katas, along with information on sparring drills and karate competitions.
ISBN-13: 978-1-55407-396-2 (pbk.)
ISBN-10: 1-55407-396-0 (pbk.)
1. Karate. 2. Karate — Training. I. Title.
796.815/3 dc22   GV1114.3.M378 2008

Library and Archives Canada Cataloguing in Publication

Martin, Ashley P., 1972-
   Advanced Shotokan karate : black belt and beyond / Ashley P. Martin.
Includes bibliographical references and index.
ISBN-13: 978-1-55407-396-2
ISBN-10: 1-55407-396-0
   1. Karate. 2. Karate — Training. I. Title.
GV1114.3.M376 2008   796.815'3   C2008-901223-2

Note: It is always the responsibility of the individual to assess his or her own fitness capability before participating in any training activity. Whilst every effort has been made to ensure the content of this book is as technically accurate as possible, neither the author nor the publishers can accept responsibility for any injury or loss sustained as a result of the use of this material.

Published in the United States by
Firefly Books (U.S.) Inc.
P.O. Box 1338, Ellicott Station
Buffalo, New York 14205

Published in Canada by
Firefly Books Ltd.
66 Leek Crescent
Richmond Hill, Ontario L4B 1H1

Typeset in 9.5/13.75pt MetaPlusNormal by Margaret Brain
Text and cover design by James Watson
Printed and bound in China

Contents

CHAPTER **ONE** introduction

This book is intended as a guide for the advanced karate student, from brown belt level and through the first few years as a black belt. It builds on the material presented in *The Shotokan Karate Bible* (see Bibliography) and contains the knowledge that a first-degree black belt (shodan) needs to possess in order to progress to the second-degree black belt level (nidan). Studying from a book is no substitute for a good teacher, but it can complement training in the dojo.

Beyond Black Belt

Acquiring the black belt is not the end of your karate training. The black belt levels continue beyond the first degree as shown below.

BLACK BELT LEVELS	
Dan	*Level name*
1st	shodan
2nd	nidan
3rd	sandan
4th	yondan
5th	godan
6th	rokudan
7th	sichidan
8th	hachidan
9th	kudan
10th	judan

In some karate organizations, the highest dan grades wear a different-colored belt, for example a red and black belt. However, in most karate schools, there are no new belt colors for the advanced student and all the dan grades wear the black belt. It is, however, often possible to identify a more advanced student. Most black belts are actually made of white cotton and are simply wrapped in black silk. Each time the belt is put on and taken off, a small amount of silk is worn away. Over the years this can result in the belt losing its black color and becoming increasingly white.

A silk black belt with Shotokan karatedo *embroidered onto it in kanji*

A silk black belt that has been worn away through many years of use

Some karate practitioners put tags on their black belt to indicate their rank, or have their rank written on the belt, either in their native language or in Japanese characters.

The Advanced Karate Syllabus

The syllabus to reach the first-degree black belt level is listed in the Appendices and covered in detail in *The Shotokan Karate Bible*. The syllabus to progress to second-degree black belt (nidan) is summarized below and explained in detail in this book. The basics (kihon) vary from organization to organization, but are essentially the same as the previous level with the addition of some double-kick combinations. Sparring (kumite) follows the same form as the previous level, but of course you will be expected to perform with greater skill. The primary difference is the kata. You will be expected to know all of the brown belt kata and, in addition, you will need to learn one of the first dan optional kata.

The best kata to choose for your second dan grading will depend on your specific strengths and preferences, but Nijushiho is generally recommended. This offers a good balance of new techniques and dynamic moves while not being overly athletic in its demands.

BLACK BELT GRADING SYLLABUS, 1ST DAN TO 2ND DAN	
Basics	
Triple punch	Kizami-zuki, oi-zuki, gyaku-zuki
Front kick combination	Mae-geri, oi-zuki, gyaku-zuki
Side thrusting kick combination	Yoko kekomi, uraken-uchi, gyaku-zuki
Roundhouse kick combination	Mawashi-geri, uraken-uchi, gyaku-zuki
Back kick combination	Ushiro-geri, uraken-uchi, gyaku-zuki
Front kick/roundhouse kick combination	Mae-geri, mawashi-geri, uraken-uchi, gyaku-zuki
Roundhouse kick/side thrusting kick combination	Mawashi-geri, yoko kekomi, uraken-uchi, gyaku-zuki
Roundhouse kick/reverse-back roundhouse kick combination	Mawashi-geri, ushiro ura mawashi-geri, uraken-uchi, gyaku-zuki
Front kick/back kick combination	Mae-geri, ushiro-geri, uraken-uchi, gyaku-zuki

Four-kick combination	Mae-geri, move front foot back, yoko kekomi, mawashi-geri, ushiro-geri, uraken-uchi, gyaku-zuki
Standing kicks	Mae-geri, yoko kekomi, ushiro-geri, mawashi-geri
Shodan combination	Mae-geri, oi-zuki, gyaku-zuki, step back gedan barai, gyaku-zuki, mawashi geri, uraken-uchi, oi-zuki

Kata

Kihon Kata (Taikyoku Shodan)

Heian Shodan

Heian Nidan

Heian Sandan

Heian Yondan

Heian Godan

Tekki Shodan

Bassai Dai

Kanku Dai

Jion

Empi

Hangetsu

Choose one from:

Bassai Sho, Kanku Sho, Jitte, Nijushiho, Tekki Nidan

Kumite

One-step free sparring	Jiyu ippon kumite
Head-level stepping punch	Jodan oi-zuki
Stomach-level stepping punch	Chudan oi-zuki
Front kick	Mae-geri
Side thrusting kick	Yoko kekomi
Roundhouse kick	Mawashi-geri
Back kick	Ushiro-geri
Free sparring	Jiyu kumite

The Shotokan Kata List

For all gradings below fifth dan, there is an optional kata list from which the candidate must choose one kata to perform and a compulsory list from which the examiner may select any for the candidate to perform. Those grading to fifth dan or above are expected to know all the Shotokan kata.

Compulsory kata are sometimes called shitei (assigned) kata. This is the name often given to the kata you're asked to perform in the early elimination rounds of kata competitions.

Optional kata are sometimes called tokui (specialty) kata. This should be the kata that you have focused on and practiced the most. As a lower grade, you probably wouldn't have had a specialty kata. If you did, it was probably Bassai Dai – the kata you needed to pass your brown belt gradings. As an advanced student, you will be expected to choose a specialty kata that particularly interests you or that suits your particular strengths. In kata competitions, the later rounds are often decided on the basis of your tokui kata.

OPTIONAL AND COMPULSORY KATA
Compulsory for 1st Dan and Above
Heian Shodan
Heian Nidan
Heian Sandan
Heian Yondan
Heian Godan
Tekki Shodan

Optional for 1st Dan; Compulsory for 2nd Dan and Above
Bassai Dai
Kanku Dai
Jion
Empi
Hangetsu
Optional for 2nd Dan; Compulsory for 3rd Dan and Above
Bassai Sho
Kanku Sho
Jitte
Nijushiho
Tekki Nidan
Optional for 3rd Dan; Compulsory for 4th Dan and Above
Chinte
Gankanku
Gojushiho Sho
Sochin
Unsu
Optional for 4th Dan; Compulsory for 5th Dan and Above
Gojushiho Dai
Ji'in
Meikyo
Tekki Sandan
Wankan

The Advanced Student

It is sometimes said that Shotokan karate trains the "best white belts" in the world, but this is not meant as a compliment. It is instead intended to imply that Shotokan black belts are no more than very highly trained white belts and are performing their karate in a slightly naive fashion. As a black belt, you should not simply be doing the same karate as white belts, even if it is at a higher intensity and with greater precision.

THE DIFFERENCE BETWEEN AN ADVANCED KARATE STUDENT AND A BEGINNER	
Novice	*Advanced Student*
Does what he or she is told	Questions dogma
Follows black and white rules	Modifies behavior in response to complex changes in circumstances
Mainly works on the next grading kata	Has many kata to maintain, and specializes in one or two
Can perform simple combinations with practice	Can quickly learn complex combinations and create effective new combinations
Understanding of kata is based on careful imitation and repetition	Understanding of kata is enhanced by knowledge of practical kata applications

LEARN TO BREAK THE RULES

Lower grades are given rules to follow, for example "keep your heels down," "keep your back straight" and "rotate the fist at the end of a punch." Under examination, some of these dogmatic rules don't appear to make sense all of the time. For example, boxers don't seem to follow these rules, but they can punch and defend effectively. But how can this be? Surely the methods and traditions of karate cannot be wrong?

What you need to understand is that some of the instructions given to lower grades are there to prohibit bad habits and aren't really absolute rules. It requires a deeper understanding of karate to distinguish between the rules that need to be followed and those that don't. These gray areas are confusing for a white belt – that's why a relatively simple and straightforward rule set is presented to beginners. As a black belt, you should understand when it's appropriate to break these rules.

The Old Martial Way of Okinawa

Many karate schools include some traditional weapons training under the label of Okinawan kobudo, which means the "old martial way of Okinawa."

TRADITIONAL WEAPONS OF OKINAWA	
Name	**Description**
bo	Six-foot wooden staff
sai	Three-pronged metal dagger
tonfa	Baton about two feet long with a handle. Forerunner of the modern police baton
nunchaku	Two-section staff. Two sticks connected by a short chain or rope.

Many karate schools include training with the bo, the six-foot staff

Training using weapons can help with your understanding of empty-handed techniques. This is because the weapon forms use the same principles as the empty-handed forms, but the added weight of the weapons mean that if you perform a technique inefficiently using bad form, you will quickly become tired.

Cross-Training

Cross-training in the world of martial arts is sometimes thought of as a recent phenomenon brought about by the popularity of Ultimate Fighting Championships and mixed martial arts. However, the idea of training in different martial arts in order to produce a more rounded fighting style is not new. Part of Bruce Lee's combat philosophy, Jeet Kune Do, was to break free from the limitations of one style of fighting. He said:

The best fighter is not a Boxer, Karate or Judo man. The best fighter is someone who can adapt to any style. He kicks too good for a Boxer, throws too good for a Karate man and punches too good for a Judo man.

The great classical karate masters were no strangers to the idea of cross-training. In the early days of karate, there was a continual interchange of techniques between different karate masters.

As a beginner, it is important to focus on one martial art. All the different elements of Shotokan reinforce each other using consistent themes and consistent rules. Dabbling in other martial arts can be confusing for the beginner, but a broader view can be enlightening for the advanced student. If you do five different martial arts or karate styles for a year each, you will end up following five beginner's courses and go away with the skills of someone who has done one year of training. If you focus on one martial art first for five years before cross-training, you'll understand how to integrate the new knowledge into your five years of experience, thereby improving the quality of your karate. Again, it's Bruce Lee who says it best:

I fear not the man who has practiced 10,000 kicks once, but I fear the man who has practiced one kick 10,000 times.

There are valuable lessons to be learned from the other styles of karate. The early Shotokan karate masters understood this and went to train under Kenwa Mabuni, the founder of Shito-ryu. This resulted in the kata Unsu, Sochin and Nijushiho being imported into the Shotokan system. It is worth taking a look at the Shito-ryu version of these kata as well as some of the other major Goju-ryu kata such as Seipei and Seienchin. Other styles also have slightly different versions of the Shotokan kata and these can be worth studying. Over the years, some of the kata have been misremembered, and studying sibling styles of karate can help to reconstruct the original intention of the kata creator and make more sense of some of the more obscure movements. This is not to say that innovation in karate is a bad thing. In fact, it is essential for the continued evolution of the art.

The grappling martial arts like jiu jitsu, judo and aikido are great for finding out about locks, holds and throws. These kinds of techniques are rarely covered in karate classes but are essential if you want to truly understand the karate kata.

Interpreting Kata

For most karate students, it is enough to simply learn the kata movements without any understanding of what all those movements are actually used for. If you're only interested in passing gradings and winning competitions, this is all you need to know. But there has been an increasing trend toward understanding the applications

of kata sequences at a deeper level and a dissatisfaction with the overly simplistic and unrealistic explanations that have been provided in recent history.

Defenses should be against attacks that would realistically be used by an untrained assailant, not against formal karate-style attacks. Someone on the street is unlikely to attack with a straight stepping punch (oi-zuki) or any sort of kick above waist height.

The karate kata contain techniques that are effective at many different ranges. Modern karate practitioners tend to see everything as being in the medium to long range, which is what you see in karate competitions. In the kata, usually only the initial move is at that range and then all the rest are at close range.

Opponents on the ground can be finished off with a punch, but it is better to use a stamp, a kick, an arm-lock submission or a throat hold.

Slow moves often indicate strong grappling moves, using strength and leverage to break a grip or apply a lock or hold. Slow moves in kata are typically performed faster at the beginning and then with decreasing speed and increasing tension. This reflects the reality of applying a grappling move: first, you need to grab your opponent, which should be done quickly, but then as you apply the lock or hold you are working against bones and connective tissue.

Structure of This Book

This section presents short summaries of the topics covered in more detail later in the book.

CHAPTER 2 – HISTORY OF KARATE

You don't need to know the origins of karate to be a successful karate black belt, but the mysterious and ancient origins of the oriental martial arts are a key attraction for many pursuing a traditional martial art like karate.

Most people think of karate as a Japanese martial art with traditions that go back hundreds, if not thousands, of years. But in fact karate was as novel and exotic to the Japanese when it was first taught in the Tokyo universities in the 1920s as it was to Westerners when karate was brought to Europe and the United States in the 1950s and 1960s. Today, most instructors make every effort to preserve the ancient traditions of karate. But a mere hundred years ago, karate would have been considered a revolutionary new style of unarmed fighting and it would not have been uncommon for karate masters to invent their own kata.

Shotokan karate evolved directly from a system of unarmed fighting developed by the royal bodyguards to the King of Okinawa. All the styles of karate have their origins in the Chinese martial arts that have been practiced in Okinawa for centuries. However, it was not until the 19th century that the key developments were made by the masters of the Okinawan fighting arts based in the royal city of Shuri, developments which would lead ultimately to the karate style that today we call Shotokan. The main contributors to this new style of fighting were Sokon Matsumura, who was chief bodyguard to the King of Okinawa, and Anko Itosu, who also worked in the royal court.

Karate became a Japanese art in the 20th century when Gichin Funakoshi introduced karate to Japan. Since then, karate has enjoyed rapid growth in the modern world, its popularity fueled by modern innovations such as karate tournaments and martial arts movies.

CHAPTER 3 – BASIC FORM

One of the main distinguishing features of the advanced student is the ability to use leg techniques effectively. Kicks can be the most impressive aspects of karate, but they require the most strength, coordination and flexibility. The advanced level combinations consist of a number of double-kick combinations that are intended to refine your kicking abilities.

Remember that it is essential that you still work to refine the basic form you learned before becoming a black belt. This is especially important if, like many black belts, you are involved in teaching.

CHAPTERS 4 TO 9 – KATA

Origins

Most kata in the Shotokan system can be attributed to Sokon Matsumura or Anko Itosu. They were either based on kata that had come to Matsumura and Itosu from China or were invented by them.

The origins sections of these chapters discuss the meaning of the name of the kata. In many cases, the kata have been passed down using the oral tradition and their names were never written down. Without knowing the Japanese kanji for the kata name, we can only guess at the meaning of the name. For example, Jion is written as two characters. The first character could be written using the character for "temple," or using the character for "love." The second character could be written using either "mercy" or "sound." Whichever characters are used, it is still pronounced "Jion," but the name could mean "temple of love," "temple sound" or "mercy of love."

Importance

These sections explain how the kata fits in with the other Shotokan kata. Some kata, such as Kanku Dai, share many similarities with other kata in the Shotokan system, meaning that many sequences will already be familiar even if Kanku Dai is new for you. Other kata, such as Nijushiho, stand out as being quite unique. While this might mean that learning the kata is more challenging, since there is no familiar territory it can also make the kata more novel and interesting.

Performance Tips

Simply running through the moves of the kata is sometimes not enough. These sections explain how the kata should be performed. For example, some sequences are better performed in combination, leaving only small gaps between the techniques.

New Techniques

These sections introduce important new techniques that haven't been covered in previous kata.

Kata Sequence

These sections run through the kata step by step, breaking down complicated moves where appropriate. The numbers indicate the moves that would be made to each count in class, with sub-moves being indicated with a letter. For example, the first move in Bassai Dai is shown in two steps, 1a and 1b. These steps should be performed as one complete movement.

Variations

Today, practitioners are strict about maintaining the traditions of karate and adhering to the kata sequence that was passed down to them. It was not always this way. Before the 20th century, it was common practice for karate masters to make kata their own by introducing major modifications or even creating entirely new kata of their own. With the advent of big karate organizations, karate rank exams and kata competitions, fixed standards became increasingly important. Any variation from the established way of performing a kata in a grading will often lead to failing that exam, and in a kata competition it will result in lost points.

Variations do, however, still exist, and some of the major ones are highlighted in these sections. Sometimes high-ranking practitioners make modifications to improve the kata. In some cases, the variation may in fact be the old way that has gone out of fashion. Variations also come about by accident, with karate masters misremembering the kata and those "mistakes" being picked up and then popularized by their students. It is important to remember that these variations are not necessarily any worse than the standard way of performing the kata.

CHAPTER 10 – SPARRING DRILLS

The sparring drills in these sections are not fixed sequences required for grading, but instead are useful combinations that can be practiced in order to improve your sparring.

CHAPTER 11 – KARATE COMPETITIONS

Competitions are not part of karate's traditional heritage but are a relatively recent innovation. However, karate would not enjoy the success it does today if it were not for karate competitions, which are a great attraction and motivator for many participants. These sections explain how competitions are typically organized, how points are awarded and some of the terminology used.

CHAPTER **TWO** history of karate

Much of the history of karate is shrouded in mystery. This is sometimes explained as being a consequence of the fact that, before the 20th century, martial arts were often practiced in secret societies. But a more significant factor seems to have been the impact of the "Typhoon of Steel," the invasion of Okinawa in 1945 by American forces that completely flattened the cities of Naha and Shuri, destroying any written records of karate's early development.

An examination of the available details suggests a fascinating origin for karate in Okinawa: a crack team of royal bodyguards, a kind of 19th-century secret service, working as bureaucrats and palace officials by day, and developing and practicing a deadly unarmed fighting style by night.

KARATE TIMELINE	
1429	Okinawa unified. Weapons banned.
1609	Japanese Satsuma clan invades Okinawa
1853	Commodore Perry visits Okinawa
1901	Karate first taught in an Okinawan school
1916	Karate first demonstrated on mainland Japan
1934	Chojun Miyagi visits Hawaii
1948	Formation of the Japan Karate Association (JKA)
1957	First JKA karate championship

Chinese Way of the Fist

Many accounts of the origin of karate trace its roots back to ancient China with the introduction of martial exercises into the Shaolin temple by a Buddhist monk called Bodhidharma in the sixth century. He traveled from India to the Shaolin temple in China and found the resident monks to be in a feeble condition. Bodhidharma instructed the monks in the courtyard and began to teach them in the art of Shih Pa Lohan Sho (the 18 hands of Lohan) so that the monks could attain spiritual enlightenment while preserving their physical health.

This story may be more myth than history, but the Shaolin temple was certainly one source of the class of Chinese martial arts known as ch'uan fa, the "way of the fist." Chinese ch'uan fa was certainly a major influence on the martial art that we call karate today. But few of the Chinese traditions have been continued by karate practitioners and so, to find the real birthplace of karate, we need to look at a small island in the East China Sea called Okinawa.

Karate: An Okinawan Martial Art

Okinawa is the largest of the Ryukyu Islands, an island chain that extends about 600 miles (1,000 km) from southern Japan to Taiwan. Today, Okinawa Island is the capital of the Japanese Okinawa Prefecture, but it was once an independent nation with a separate language and culture.

The Ryukyu Islands are located in the East China Sea

Martial arts probably existed in Okinawa as early as the Chinese Tang Dynasty (AD 618–906), but they would have been quite different from the karate that we see today. Okinawa entered into a tributary relationship with China in 1372, which accelerated Chinese influences on Okinawan culture. There was a permanent Chinese mission resident in the Okinawan Royal Palace, and many of the officials brought with them ch'uan fa secrets. At this stage, it would have been a distinctly Chinese martial art.

KARATE: A PEASANTS' MARTIAL ART?

A common misconception is that karate was started in Okinawa by peasants.

Learning a martial art like karate takes a great deal of time and effort. Peasants spent all of their time during the day working, often doing back-breaking work – it would take an extraordinary person to then engage in something as physically demanding as karate in the evening. In fact, the karate masters were invariably of the keimochi (noble) class.

Three cities on Okinawa are important to the story of karate's development: Naha, a large port; Tomari, a smaller port; and the royal city of Shuri, the capital city of Okinawa. Each city had karate masters with their own kata and traditions.

The karate that developed at Naha, known as Naha-te, can be characterized as a soft-style martial art, using more circular hand and foot movements that flow from one to another giving it a graceful appearance.

Karate that follows the Shuri-te tradition is described as a hard-style martial art and tends to use big, strong, linear movements. In the 1500s, the King Sho Shen had a castle built in Shuri, to act as his palace and the bureaucratic center of his kingdom. It was here that the linear karate, which would become Shotokan karate, developed.

The Tomari traditions were rather similar to the Shuri traditions, largely due to the fact that many of the Tomari masters were originally from Shuri, having retired from royal service.

THE STYLES OF KARATE		
Style of Karate	**Founder**	**In the Tradition of**
Shotokan	Gichin Funakoshi	Shuri-te
Goju-ryu	Chogun Miyagi	Naha-te
Shito-ryu	Kenwa Mabuni	Shuri-te and Naha-te

Naha-te and Shuri-te have quite different histories and origins. Our interest is in the development of Shotokan karate and so our attention will focus on the events that unfolded in Shuri.

Two key incidents made Okinawa a unique breeding ground for a new martial art:

■ In 1429, Okinawa was unified under the first Sho Dynasty. Prior to this, Okinawa had suffered from internal conflict between warring clans. To help maintain order, the second Sho King, Sho Shin, disarmed the bickering warlords by introducing a weapons ban. The nobility, the keimochi, were instead set to work as bureaucrats.

■ In 1609, the Japanese Satsuma Clan of Kyushu invaded Okinawa. They probably found the weapons ban quite convenient and ordered that it be continued. Now, however, the ban was enforced by the Satsuma Samurai, who wielded deadly katana.

By 1650, the Japanese were operating a policy of national seclusion, Sakoku, which barred Westerners from trading in Japan (with an exception for limited trade with the Dutch). This policy was extended to Okinawa. Officially, Okinawa was still a province of China and so, to keep control of Okinawa while avoiding war with China, the Shuri officials were ordered to deny any connection with Japan.

To compound this situation, European and American ships started appearing on the Okinawan shores in the 19th century in the form of explorers, missionaries and whalers. This conflicted with Japanese isolationism and put the officials at Shuri in a difficult and dangerous position. They were instructed not to allow trade with the Westerners, but were also not permitted to explain that the King of Okinawa was subordinate to the Japanese.

Matters came to a head in 1853 when Commodore Matthew Perry of the United States Navy paid a visit to Okinawa. His objective was to open trade between Japan and the United States. Perry decided that a show of strength in Okinawa was needed as a prelude to his negotiations in Japan itself. He demanded that he be allowed to see the King to discuss a trade agreement. As usual, the Okinawan officials politely declined. Perry then landed a force of 200 marines armed with Springfield rifled muskets, two cannons and two brass bands, and paraded up to Shuri castle. Perry himself traveled on a sedan chair carried by Chinese coolies.

Perry and his entourage marched up to the gates of the royal palace and demanded entry. The Shuri officials allowed him into the main hall, where he found the Regent and a small group of his staff. The Okinawans expected Perry to declare himself governor of Okinawa, but Perry had only planned to demonstrate his strength and, having made his point, he returned to his ship. It was a tense incident nonetheless, and coming face to face with 200 marines must have had an impact on the staff at Shuri. And, as so many of the karate masters of that day were employed as high-ranking members of the Royal household, it is very likely that they would have been there facing Perry and his men.

B.D. Clayton suggests that this encounter at Shuri Castle, combined perhaps with the many presumed incidents that remain undocumented, had a fundamental influence on the development of karate. He suggests that karate was designed to deal with a "target rich" environment, which is to say that it is meant to be effective even when you are outnumbered and surrounded by opponents. He concludes the following:

■ Spending more than a few seconds fighting each opponent would not be good enough – they would have to be dispatched very rapidly

■ Ground fighting would be suicide

■ Defending against opponents armed with firearms or swords was necessary.

SATUNISHI "TODE" SAKUGAWA (1733–1815)

Sakugawa studied under an Okinawan master of tode called Takahara. He learned White Crane–style ch'uan fa from Kong Su Kung, the Chinese military attaché to the Okinawan court. (The name of the Chinese dignitary who trained Sakugawa is a matter of controversy: Kong Su Kung might not have been his name, but instead his rank.)

The Okinawan reading of the ideographs of Kong Su Kung can be read Kushanku and Sakugawa is often credited with having created the kata Kushanku, which would later form the basis of the Shotokan kata Kanku

Dai and Kanku Sho. In Shotokan karate, Kanku Dai is the "master" kata. It appears to contain segments from all the core Shotokan kata and may well have been the precursor of the Heian kata.

Sakugawa is sometimes credited with creating the dojo kun, the school code, but more commonly it is attributed instead to Gichin Funakoshi. The dojo kun is recited in many karate schools to this day. Its most literal translation reads:

Each seek perfection of character
Each protect the way of truth
Each foster the spirit of effort
Each respect others
Each guard against impetuous courage.

Perhaps Sakugawa's greatest legacy was his most famous student, Sokon Matsumura.

SOKON "BUSHI" MATSUMURA (1797–1893)

The Bodyguard

If there was one man responsible for the transformation of Okinawa-te from what was essentially a Chinese art to the new art of karate, it was Sokon Matsumura.

Matsumura started training with Sakugawa at the age of 14. He was determined to become the greatest fighter in the land. He went on to become master of military affairs in the royal court, a highly important position, as it would have meant that he was responsible for the safety of the King. After the capture of Okinawa by the Satsuma Clan, the King was required to spend half the year in Kyushu. Naturally, Matsumura traveled with the King and it was during this time that Matsumura learned the sword fighting art of Jigen Ryu Kenjutsu.

Legend has it that Matsumura was given the title Bushi, meaning warrior, by the King Sho Ko after he fought a bull unarmed. The King had announced that, as entertainment, his great bodyguard, Matsumura, would battle a raging bull (some accounts say that the bull was a present from the Emperor of Japan). Everyone was invited to watch the great spectacle. Matsumura had no choice but to accept the challenge or lose face. On the appointed day, he turned up to face the bull. He stared into the bull's eyes and it turned around and bolted. He had defeated the bull just by looking at it!

Matsumura had accomplished this apparent miracle by careful preparation. On discovering the impossible task he had been set, he went to visit the bull, taking with him a long pin. He looked into the eyes of the bull and poked it on the nose. He repeated this every day, up to the day of the challenge. He thus trained the bull to fear his gaze and so actually won through careful planning.

Over time, Matsumura served as chief bodyguard to a total of three Okinawan kings: King Sho Ko, King Sho Iku and King Sho Tai. All three were deposed by their Japanese masters. The last, Sho Tai, was ousted at the beginning of the Meiji Restoration when the Kingdom of Ryukyu became the Okinawa Prefecture. Sho Tai was abducted and taken to Japan, where he lived out his final days in exile. The aristocracy was abolished and this would have put Matsumura and all the other Shuri officials out of work.

Matsumura would have been in service at the time that Perry made his historic visit to Shuri and, given his position, it is quite likely that he would have been in that hall, standing at the Regent's side and facing 200 marines. This event may have influenced the direction of Matsumura's training and so have helped shape modern karate.

ANKO ITOSU (1830–1915)

The Big Kata Man

Itosu worked alongside Matsumura as secretary and translator to the King of Okinawa. But he was also, presumably, an apprentice bodyguard to the King under Matsumura. He trained and worked alongside Matsumura for 30 years.

Itosu was heavily built and had a reputation for being very strong and for being able to withstand heavy blows.

G. Funakoshi says that he had "the silhouette of a barrel" and that he could crush bamboo with his bare hands.

In 1901, Itosu introduced karate into the physical education system at an elementary school in Shuri. This was the same year that King Sho Tai died in exile and it is possible that this was no coincidence. Once there was no chance that the King would return, perhaps Itosu felt released from any vows of secrecy he had taken while a royal bodyguard.

In 1908, he wrote a letter to the Prefecture Educational Department outlining the benefits that karate had to offer and encouraging the introduction of karate into all Okinawan schools. His suggestion was well received and karate became part of the school curriculum in Okinawa. This made karate instruction available to the masses for the first time: the veil of secrecy over karate had been well and truly lifted.

Itosu's greatest legacy is his contribution to karate kata. He decided that some relatively easy kata were needed for teaching to middle school students. He invented the Pinan kata, which in the Shotokan system are known as the Heian kata. These kata were possibly based on the Kanku kata combined with moves from a long forgotten kata called Chanan. Other kata that Itosu is reputed to have created are Naifanchi Nidan and Naifanchi Sandan, which later became known as Tekki Nidan and Tekki Sandan. An alternative theory is that the three Tekki kata were originally one long kata and that Itosu split them up. He also standardized the versions of Kanku Sho and Kanku Dai that are based on the kata Kushanku.

ANKO AZATO (1828–1906)

The Invisible Man of Karate

It seems that there are no surviving pictures of Azato and very little is written about him, which makes him a bit of a mystery man. Most of what we know comes from the writings of Gichin Funakoshi, who referred to Azato as the best martial artist he had ever met.

Like Itosu, Azato was one of Matsumura's students and held the position of foreign affairs advisor within the Shuri Royal Court. He was a member of the aristocracy. He owned a castle and was a hereditary lord of the Azato village.

Funakoshi tells us that Azato challenged an armed sword master to a duel and defeated him with his bare hands by deflecting the sword with his arm before immobilizing his opponent. In another story, Azato and Itosu were confronted by 30 men and so they fled into a nearby house. The men swarmed around the house and the two decided that a fight was unavoidable. Azato leaped out of the window and started dispatching one hoodlum after another using a single blow each time, while Itosu dealt with the men around the other side of the house.

What is notable about this story is that it mentions that Azato and Itosu were using what is today called ikken hissatsu, one deadly strike, which represents the ability to defeat an opponent with a single devastating attack. This is one of the defining characteristics of modern Shotokan karate.

Karate: A Japanese Martial Art

GICHIN "SHOTO" FUNAKOSHI (1868–1957)

The Father of Japanese Karate

Gichin Funakoshi was the school teacher from Shuri who is credited with bringing karate to Japan, thus earning himself the title of "Father of Modern Karate" (or sometimes "Father of Japanese Karate"). In fact, he wasn't alone in bringing karate to Japan. Many karate masters from Okinawa traveled to Japan to promote their art, including Kenwa Mabuni, founder of Shito-ryu, which is a synthesis of Shuri-te and Naha-te, and Chojun Miyagi, founder of Goju-ryu, which is based on the Naha-te traditions. But it was Funakoshi who did it first and perhaps did the better job of promoting it.

Funakoshi started learning karate under Anko Azato and later studied under Itosu. He recalls that he spent 10 years learning the three Naihanchi (Tekki) kata under Itosu.

In 1913, as chairman of the Shobukai, the martial arts association of Okinawa, Funakoshi organized a group to travel around Okinawa performing public demonstrations of karate. It wasn't until 1916 that he was able to take karate to Japan, where he demonstrated at the Butokuden, the official center of Japanese martial arts. This event, and the demonstrations that followed, helped to bolster the popularity of the art. However, it was the visit of the Crown Prince of Japan, Hirohito, that really raised the profile of karate and, in 1922, Funakoshi was invited by the Japanese Education Ministry to demonstrate karate at the first All Japan Athletic Exhibition in Tokyo. During his time in Japan, he stayed as a guest of Jigoro Kano, the creator of judo, and taught at the Kodokan, the judo school.

At the time that Funakoshi brought karate to Japan, the country was going through a very nationalistic phase and anything that was not considered to be purely Japanese was regarded with suspicion or contempt. Karate, of course, was of Chinese and Okinawan origin. To overcome this perception, Funakoshi portrayed karate as following the Japanese budo (martial) tradition and made the following changes:

- The first ideograph in kara-te was changed from the old one that represented China to a new one meaning "empty."

- Funakoshi adopted the uniforms and belt system of Kano's judo. Before this, there was no such thing as a karate black belt.

- Chinese culture was viewed with suspicion, but Zen Buddhism was not. Zen had a great deal of influence on Japanese culture and was considered an important part of Japanese budo. Karate's Shaolin origins were therefore emphasized, and the Zen-like

kara ideograph was adopted, thus associating karate with Zen Buddhism. This link was somewhat spurious since karate's development had so long been tied to Okinawa, which had never really adopted Buddhism in the same way as Japan.

- Funakoshi attempted to change the kata names to Japanese words. For example, he renamed the Naihanchi kata "Tekki," but only a few of these new names persisted into the next generation of karate instructors, Funakoshi's own son included. Perhaps for them the exotic Chinese or Okinawan names just had more flavor than (from their point of view) the mundane Japanese-sounding names.

SHOTOKAN KATA NAMES

Okinawan/ Chinese Name	Funakoshi's New Japanese Name	Modern Shotokan Name
Pinan	Heian	Heian
Naihanchi	Tekki	Tekki
Seisan	Hangetsu	Hangetsu
Chinto	Gankaku	Gankaku
Niseishi	Nijushiho	Nijushiho
Wanshu	Empi	Empi
Rohai	Meikyo	Meikyo
Useishi	Hotaku	Gojushiho
Ji'in	Shokyo	Ji'in
Sochin	Hakko	Sochin
Chinte	Shoin	Chinte

Funakoshi invented the Taikyoku Kata and Ten No Kata, which were even simpler versions of Itosu's Pinan (Heian) kata for teaching to elementary school students. However, according to one of Funakoshi's students, Shigeru Egami, these kata were in fact created by Funakoshi's son, Yoshitaka.

By 1935, Funakoshi had sufficient financial backing to build the first karate dojo, or training hall, in Japan. It became known as the Shotokan, after Funakoshi's pen name, "shoto" literally meaning "pine waves," and "kan," meaning "house."

YOSHITAKA "GIGO" FUNAKOSHI (1906–1945)

The Young Teacher

Gichin Funakoshi started the transformation of karate from an Okinawan to a Japanese art, but these changes were primarily ones of philosophy and nomenclature. However, Funakoshi's son, Yoshitaka (or Gigo, using a different reading of the ideographs for his name), really did transform the techniques of karate to produce what is essentially the Shotokan karate that we practice today.

At a very young age, Yoshitaka was diagnosed as having tuberculosis, a terrible disease that, in 1913, was effectively a death sentence. Despite this, he engaged in his karate practice with great energy and spirit. He used very low, long stances and had a great love of sparring. He is said to have been responsible for the introduction of the side kicks, yoko kekomi and yoko keage, and the roundhouse kick, mawashi-geri, into the Shotokan karate system.

The two Funakoshis shared the teaching at the Shotokan. The softly spoken Gichin would teach his karate with high stances in the afternoon. The spirited and outspoken Yoshitaka, who was referred to by the students as waka sensei, young teacher, would teach his low stances, big punches and high kicks in the evening. Yoshitaka sadly succumbed to a lung infection in 1945 and died. Despite this, it is clear that it is Yoshitaka's method that lives on in modern Shotokan karate.

Following the Second World War, the occupying American forces placed a ban on martial arts in Japan because they were thought to have fostered regimentation and militarism. Karate managed to continue largely due to its emphasis on being a "do," a way of life, which had spiritual goals and positive health applications rather than militaristic objectives.

As it turned out, the occupying forces weren't to be the end of karate but instead a great force in popularizing it. There was a great deal of interest in karate from servicemen stationed in Japan, and many of them trained with karate schools there and then took this strange new art back to their home countries.

How the West Was Won

The period after the Second World War saw growing fascination in the West with all things Oriental. But karate still remained relatively unknown. In Ian Fleming's *Goldfinger*, first published in 1959, Goldfinger says to James Bond:

Have you ever heard of karate? No? Well that man is one of the three men in the world that have achieved the black belt in karate.

Fleming's view is that Bond, who is described as an expert in unarmed fighting, wouldn't have heard of karate. This tells us just how obscure karate must have been in 1959, which seems extraordinary today with every town having multiple karate clubs and terms such as karate kick or karate chop part of everyday language.

The first public demonstrations of karate in the United States took place in Hawaii, where there was already a large population of Japanese and Okinawans. A number of masters of Okinawan karate visited Hawaii in the 1920s and 1930s. The most notable was Chojun Miyagi, founder of the Goju-ryu style of karate, who remained in Hawaii from May 1934 until January 1935. His classes were marketed as "kempo karate." Kempo is the Japanese reading of the characters for the Chinese ch'uan fa, the way of the fist.

The kempo karate "brand" was later reused by the Hawaiian-born William Chow (1914–1987). Chow studied Koshu Ryu Kempo under James Mitose and it is important to understand that this was very much a Chinese art, not to be confused with the uniquely Okinawan art that Gichin Funakoshi had taken to Japan and that would become Shotokan karate. When Chojun Miyagi had referred to his art as "kempo karate," it was probably a reflection of its mixed Chinese and Okinawan heritage. Chow, however, probably used the word karate simply because, at the time, it was a more familiar term in Hawaii than kempo. The result was that karate became associated with a much broader class of martial arts than just the fighting style of Okinawa.

Of the many students that William Chow promoted to the rank of black belt, the most influential was Ed Parker, who would become known as the "Father of American Karate." Parker was born in Hawaii and was introduced to kempo in the 1940s. After receiving his black belt grade in 1953, he moved to California where he opened his first dojo in 1956. As a student of Chow, he initially called his art kempo karate, but in later years, and after further development, he renamed it "American Kempo." Parker was a gifted businessman and was a major force in promoting karate throughout the United States and Europe. He opened dojos, gave seminars and organized his International Karate Championship, which was notable for hosting the impromptu exhibition match between Bruce Lee and Chuck Norris in 1964. Parker also trained stuntmen and celebrities, including Elvis Presley, whose great interest in karate dated from his time in the U.S. army.

THE KARATE CORPORATION

One organization that contributed greatly to the popularization of traditional Shotokan karate was the Nihon Karate Kyokai – the Japan Karate Association (JKA) – which was founded in 1948 with Funakoshi named as the Chief Instructor. At that time, the JKA was based on the clubs studying Funakoshi's karate in the Tokyo area, and in fact almost all of the senior JKA members were from the university clubs of Takushoku, Waseda and Keio. Karate quickly spread under the JKA, as it actively promoted karate worldwide by sending the graduates of its instructor training program all over the world.

One of these instructors was Hidetaka Nishiyama who, in 1953, was invited by the U.S. Air Force on a sponsored tour of air bases in the mainland United States to teach special courses for the personnel. Like so many of the original JKA instructors, Nishiyama had first trained in judo and kendo. He began his karate instruction under Gichin Funakoshi, and in 1949 became captain of Takushoku University's karate team. After his move to North America, he formed the All American Karate Federation (AAKF) and would later become executive director of the International Traditional Karate Federation.

Another JKA instructor who was sent to the United States by the JKA was Teruyuki Okazaki. While Nishiyama was based in California on the west coast, Okazaki was based on the east coast, in Philadelphia. He created the East Coast Karate Association, which was initially affiliated to Nishiyama's AAKF but in 1965 broke away and formed the International Shotokan Karate Federation.

In Europe, the JKA was represented by Hirokazu Kanazawa and Keinosuke Enoeda. Kanazawa was one of the first to graduate from the JKA instructor training program and was the All Japan Karate Champion from 1957 until 1959. He became Chief Instructor of the Karate Union of Great Britain (KUGB) in 1966 before moving to Germany in 1968. Enoeda, who became known as "The Tiger," was a Takashoku graduate and winner of the All Japan Karate Championship in 1963. He took over leading the KUGB on Kanazawa's departure.

SHOTOKAN SPLITS

In 1957, Gichin Funakoshi passed away. He did not name a successor and his students split into two groups. One group called themselves Shotokai (meaning "Shoto's Group") and were led by Shigeru Egami. They were traditionalists who did not approve of the commercialization of karate or the growing popularity of competitive karate. The other group was the more radical JKA, led by Masatoshi Nakayama, who referred to their style as Shotokan. The JKA promoted competition and organized the first Japanese karate championship in 1957.

It was in 1986 that the then head of the JKA, Masatoshi Nakayama, passed away and leadership was passed to Nobuyuki Nakahara. However, his appointment was challenged by a number of JKA masters. Subsequent political infighting led to a major split, resulting in two main factions: one led by Tetsuhiko Asai, who appointed Mikio Yahara as Chief Instructor; and the other headed by Nakahara, who named Motokuni Sugiura Chief Instructor.

Following the split, legal disputes continued for many years over everything, including who could legally use the JKA name and who owned the headquarters building, the JKA Honbu. So for a period there was a peculiar situation in which two groups called themselves the JKA. In 1999, the Sugiura group won the exclusive right to the JKA name in Japan and the Asai group renamed themselves Japan Karate Shotokai (JKS).

The political infighting is largely irrelevant to the many people practicing karate throughout the world. There are too many karate associations to count, but they do broadly practice the same karate techniques and follow the same customs that were taught by Funakoshi and son in Tokyo at the beginning of the 20th century.

CHAPTER **THREE** basic form

The advanced-level combinations consist of a number of double-kick combinations that are intended to refine your kicking abilities. To perfect these kicks you will require a high degree of leg flexibility and strength, as well as the ability to coordinate the kicking action with correct hip rotation and movement of your body weight.

Remember that it is essential that you still work to refine the basic form you learned before becoming a black belt. This is especially important if, like many black belts, you are involved in teaching.

In addition to the sequences required to progress to shodan (which are detailed in *The Shotokan Karate Bible*), you will be required to perform the following sequences:

SHODAN TO NIDAN: NEW SEQUENCES	
Front kick/roundhouse kick combination	Mae-geri, mawashi-geri, uraken-uchi, gyaku-zuki
Roundhouse kick/side thrusting kick combination	Mawashi-geri, yoko kekomi, uraken-uchi, gyaku-zuki
Roundhouse kick/reverse-back roundhouse kick combination	Mawashi-geri, ushiro ura mawashi-geri, uraken-uchi, gyaku-zuki
Front kick/back kick combination	Mae-geri, ushiro-geri, uraken-uchi, gyaku-zuki
Four-kick combination	Mae-geri, move front foot back, yoko kekomi, mawashi-geri, ushiro-geri, uraken-uchi, gyaku-zuki
Standing kicks	Mae-geri, yoko kekomi, ushiro-geri, mawashi-geri

Front Kick/Roundhouse Kick Combination

Mae-geri/Mawashi-geri

Dropping the knee after finishing the front kick can generate more power for the roundhouse kick. However, keeping the knee high and instead generating power by pushing the hip forward looks better and is quicker. The front kick should be targeted at stomach level. The roundhouse kick targeted to stomach level is acceptable but, for more of a challenge, kick to head level.

1

Start in fighting stance with your left leg forward.

2

Front kick with your right leg.

3

Snap your leg back.

4

With the same leg, execute a roundhouse kick.

5

Execute a back-fist strike with your right hand.

6

Reverse punch with your left hand. Lock out the technique briefly before returning to fighting stance.

Roundhouse Kick/Side Thrusting Kick Combination

Mawashi-geri/Yoko Kekomi

Don't drop your knee after completing the roundhouse kick. Instead, keep the knee high and keep rotating the hips so that your knee crosses your center. This will put you in the ideal preparation position for the thrusting kick. The two kicks will come at your opponent from different directions and can be a way of bypassing a strong defensive guard. The roundhouse kick targeted to stomach level is acceptable but, for more of a challenge, kick to head level. The thrusting kick should be targeted at stomach level.

1

Start in fighting stance with your left leg forward.

2

Perform a roundhouse kick with your right leg.

3

Snap your foot back and bring your leg over to your left to prepare for a side thrusting kick.

4

Execute a side thrusting kick with your right leg.

5

Execute a back-fist strike with your right hand.

6

Reverse punch with your left hand. Lock out the technique briefly before returning to fighting stance.

Roundhouse Kick/Reverse-Back Roundhouse Kick Combination

Mawashi-geri/Ushiro Ura Mawashi-geri

This combination is made up of two kicks:

1 The regular roundhouse kick

2 A spinning roundhouse kick known as ushiro ura mawashi-geri, which translates as "reverse-back roundhouse kick."

REVERSE ROUNDHOUSE KICK

This kick, ura mawashi-geri, moves in a horizontal circular path just like the regular roundhouse kick, but it hooks in from the opposite side, hitting with the heel. Practice the reverse roundhouse kick with a partner and explore how this kick can be used to bypass a strong front guard.

1

Start the reverse roundhouse kick as if performing a side thrusting kick slightly off target.

2

Hook your leg in to complete the kick.

REVERSE-BACK ROUNDHOUSE KICK

This kick, ushiro ura mawashi-geri (effectively a spinning reverse roundhouse kick), is a particularly impressive-looking kick. Practice using the reverse-back roundhouse kick in combination with a regular roundhouse kick.

1

Start in fighting stance with your left leg forward.

2

Execute a roundhouse kick with your right leg.

3

Turn your body counter-clockwise and bring your right foot alongside your left foot.

4

Continue rotating and perform a reverse-back roundhouse kick with your left leg.

5

Execute a back-fist strike with your left hand.

6

Reverse punch with your right hand. Lock out the technique briefly before returning to fighting stance.

Front Kick/Back Kick Combination

Mae-geri/Ushiro-geri

This combination is performed by putting your foot back on the ground before firing off the next kick. Both of these kicks need to travel in a straight line, so ensure that your foot stays on your center line throughout the combination.

1

Start in fighting stance with your left leg forward.

2

Execute a front kick with your right leg.

3

Snap your foot back and put it back where it started.

4

Execute a back kick with your right leg.

5

Perform a back-fist strike with your right hand.

6

Reverse punch with your left hand. Lock out the technique briefly before returning to fighting stance.

Four-kick Combination

Between each kick in the combination, you should land in fighting stance. In this combination, the footwork between the first two kicks is slightly different from the four-kick combination required for shodan: you step down into fighting stance, but then slide your front foot back before proceeding to the next kick.

1

Start in fighting stance with your left leg forward.

2

Execute a front kick with your right leg and then step down into fighting stance.

3

Slide your right foot back to meet your left foot.

4

Perform a side thrusting kick with your left leg and then step down into fighting stance.

5

Execute a roundhouse kick with your right leg and then step down into fighting stance.

6

Execute a back kick with your left leg.

7

Perform a back-fist strike with your left hand.

8

Reverse punch with your right hand. Lock out the technique briefly before returning to fighting stance.

Standing Kicks

Make sure that you regain your balance between the kicks. Trying to kick while off balance will result in a weak kick. This combination extends the shodan standing kick combination by the addition of a roundhouse kick. This makes the sequence significantly more challenging. You are required to finish by stepping back to your starting position, but the motion of the roundhouse kick will tend to pull you forward.

1

Start in fighting stance with your left leg forward.

2

Execute a front kick with your right foot straight forward.

3

Without stepping down, perform a side thrusting kick with the same foot to the side.

4

Without stepping down, execute a back kick with the same foot straight back.

5

Without stepping down, execute a roundhouse kick with the same foot around to the front.

6

Return to fighting stance.

CHAPTER **FOUR** Bassai Dai

Because it is also usually required for brown belt grading examinations, Bassai Dai is one of the most universally well-known Shotokan kata. It is twice the length of the kata that precede it (Heian series and Tekki Shodan) and requires good physical fitness to perform from start to finish at full power. Bassai Dai is characterized by its distinctive "mountain punches."

Origins

Bassai, originally called Passai in Okinawa, is most often translated as "storm a fortress," but it is more likely that it means "extract from a fortress." Nobody really knows for sure what the kata name means, but I like to think that, in view of Matsumura's and Itosu's roles as royal bodyguards, they would have had rescuing the King from Shuri Castle in mind when they practiced this kata.

Bassai Dai written in kanji

There are many versions of Bassai (Masatoshi Nakayama estimated that there were hundreds), about 11 of which are still practiced today. In creating Shotokan karate, Gichin Funakoshi selected the version he considered the most effective as one of the 15 core Shotokan kata. This version of Bassai became known as Bassai Dai, with another well-known variation being referred to as Bassai Sho. Here Dai means "big" or "major" and Sho means "small" or "minor," the implication being that the Dai version should be practiced first (being one of Funakoshi's 15 core kata), while the Sho version is only considered auxiliary.

Bassai Dai was demonstrated for the first time in Japan by Gichin Funakoshi in 1922. Today it is one of the most popular kata practiced throughout the various branches of karate and is often used as the main test kata for shodan (black belt) gradings.

Importance

Bassai Dai is one of the "big four" Shotokan kata along with Jion, Kanku Dai and Empi. It contains a few combinations that are very similar to sequences in Heian Godan, and this is a common source of confusion for students. Moves 27 to 30 are exactly the same as in Heian Godan and it is all too easy to slip from one kata into the other at the end of this sequence. Moves 25 to 26 are very similar to a sequence in Heian Godan, but not quite the same, the difference being the timing of the foot movement.

New Techniques

GRASPING BLOCK

Tsukami-uke
The grasping block, also known as the tiger mouth block, is similar to the knife-hand block, but the thumb sticks out to the side and the fingers are curved in slightly.

1
Start in back stance.

2
Move your right hand up and "pick up" your left hand.

3
Turn over your right hand into a grasping block and pull down.

MOUNTAIN PUNCH

Yama-zuki

Moves 34, 36 and 38 from Bassai Dai (see pages 40 and 41) are referred to as mountain punches. They are so named because the shape of the body while doing the technique looks a bit like the Japanese kanji symbol for mountain, yama, rotated on its side.

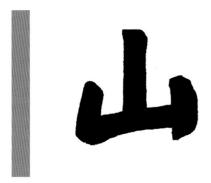

Yama, or "mountain," in kanji

The mountain punch, yama-zuki

Correct Form

1. The upper arm is slightly inclined downward.

2. The punching hands are in line, as if against a wall.

3. The lower arm is slightly inclined upward.

4. Long, narrow stance.

Kata Sequence

Bow. Announce the kata "Bassai Dai."

Start by putting your feet together and clasping your right fist in your left hand.

1a

Swing your arms back to your left side and move your weight forward ready to move.

1b

Strike forward with the back of your right fist, with your left hand placed on your right forearm. Simultaneously, step forward with your right foot and tuck your left foot behind the right.

2

Using your left foot, turn into a front stance while performing an inside block with your left hand.

3

Without stepping, block right-hand inside block.

4

Turn and block left-hand outside block.

5

Without stepping, block right-hand inside block.

6a

Bring your right foot back alongside your left and do a right-hand low-level sweeping block.

6b

Continue the sweeping movement so that your hand moves all the way up to head height.

6c

Step into a front stance with your right foot. Perform an outside block with your right arm.

7

Without stepping, block left-hand inside block.

8

Move your left foot into a shoulder-width stance and bring both of your fists to your right hip.

9

Using a slow, controlled movement, make a vertical knife-hand block with your left hand.

10

Without stepping, punch using your right hand.

11

Pull your right hand to your left shoulder and then immediately fire it forward, performing an inside block while pivoting on the spot. You should bend your knees, but your feet should simply rotate in place.

12

Straighten your legs and rotate back, squaring your hips, and punch with your left hand.

13

Pull your left hand to your right shoulder and then immediately fire it forward, performing an inside block while pivoting on the spot. You should bend your knees, but your feet should simply rotate in place.

14

Step forward with your right leg into a back stance and execute a knife-hand block.

15

Step forward with your left leg into a back stance and execute a knife-hand block.

16

Step forward with your right leg into a back stance and execute a knife-hand block.

17

Immediately, step back with your right leg into a back stance with a knife-hand block.

18

Shift into a front stance while your right hand reaches up and catches. Pull your right hand back using a grasping block.

19

Perform a low-level side thrusting kick with your right foot while your fists pull up to your ribcage. Kiai.

20

Step into a back stance and execute a knife-hand block.

21

Step forward with your right leg into a back stance and execute a knife-hand block.

22

Slowly move your right foot back to meet your left and raise both arms into a double rising block position.

23a

Abruptly, pull your arms apart and shift your weight forward.

23b

Immediately, step forward with your right foot into a front stance and strike to stomach level with a double hammer-hand strike.

Side view

24

Immediately, slide forward and punch with your right fist.

25

Turn and perform a right knife-hand strike, while blocking open-handed across your face with your left hand.

Side view

26

Slowly draw your left foot back to your right while pulling your right fist up behind your head and blocking down slowly with the left.

27

Lift your right knee and stamp down into a horse-riding stance. Simultaneously, downward block with your right hand.

Side view

28

Slowly cross and uncross your arms, blocking open-handed to your left with the back of your hand.

29

Crescent kick with your right foot into your left hand.

Side view

30

Elbow strike with your right elbow into your left hand.

Side view

31

Using a slow, controlled movement, make a vertical knife-hand block with your left hand.

32

Punch down with your left hand, bringing your right fist up to the inside of your left elbow.

33

Punch down with your right hand, bringing your left fist up to the inside of your right elbow.

Side view

34

Bring both fists to your left hip and look to the right. Step out with your right foot into a narrow front stance and attack with both fists: right fist to stomach level, left fist over your head (mountain punch).

35

Slowly, draw your right foot back to meet your left and bring both fists to your right hip.

36

Lift your left knee and step forward with a mountain punch: left fist to stomach level, right fist over your head.

37

Slowly, draw your left foot back to meet your right and bring both fists to your left hip.

38

Lift your right knee and step forward with a mountain punch: right fist to stomach level, left fist over your head.

39a

Extend your right arm up and look over your left shoulder, pulling your left hand to your hip.

39b

Turn by moving your left foot counterclockwise and swing your right arm across your body in a scooping block. Finish with a closed fist, palm side up.

40a

Extend your left arm.

40b

Pivot and swing your left arm across your body in a scooping block. Finish with a closed fist, palm side up.

41

Move your left foot to your center point and then step forward with your right foot through 45 degrees into a back stance with a knife-hand block.

42

Look over your left shoulder and then slowly move your right foot so that you rotate 90 degrees clockwise.

43

Step with your right foot to your center point and then step forward with your left foot into a back stance with a knife-hand block. Kiai.

Finish by slowly drawing your left foot back to your right and clasping your right fist in your left hand.

Variations

KNEE LIFTS (MOVES 1 AND 23B)

The Funakoshi version of Bassai Dai includes knee lifts on the moves where you launch forward. It seems that these were later removed by Nakayama. Today, both forms are common.

OUTSIDE BLOCK PREPARATION MOVE (MOVE 6C)

In Masatoshi Nakayama's definitive work on Shotokan karate, the *Best Karate* series, the preparation move for the outside block in move 6 is shown without the left hand reaching forward. However, videos of Hirokazu Kanazawa of the ISKF and Yoshiharu Osaka of the JKA show them performing this move by reaching forward with the left hand.

Performance Tips

Ensure that you use your hips on the blocking combinations at the beginning of the kata. Do not rush these combinations but ensure that individual movements are fast. A good way to do this is to group these movements in pairs, giving yourself a rest between each pair.

Bassai Dai is often described as a "big man" kata, best performed with forceful, heavy movements and best suited to big, strong practitioners. This may well have been how the heavily built "barrel shaped" Itosu would have performed this kata. Gichin Funakoshi, however, was a tiny man, being only 4 feet 11 inches tall. It seems likely that he would have provided a quite different perspective on how to perform kata. The Shotokan version of Bassai Dai contains many movements that can be interpreted as big blocking and attacking moves, and so the heavy and powerful performance works very well. Under further examination, however, the more advanced practitioner can discover ways to interpret Bassai Dai as a lighter-footed kata, with the performer skilfully twisting and turning to evade and then counterattack.

Kata Applications

GRASPING BLOCK AS A WRIST LOCK

This application is of moves 17 to 19 (see page 37). It uses the grasping block to put a lock on your opponent's wrist by trapping their hand. Use the knife-hand part of your hand as a pivot point.

This application also uses a thrusting kick to attack your opponent's knee joint. This can cause serious injury to the knee joint so, if you practice this with a partner, you must use caution.

Wrist lock

1
The attacker punches with the right hand. Use a knife-hand block to deflect the attack.

2
Use a grasping block to apply a wrist lock.

3
Lift your knee and use a side thrusting kick to attack the knee.

ARM LOCK COMBINATION

The next application is of moves 9 to 14 (see page 36). It uses the inside block action to apply an arm lock that hyperextends the elbow joint. If performed in an uncontrolled manner, this will cause damage to the ligaments and structures of the elbow, so you must use caution if you practice this with a partner.

1

The attacker grabs you.

2

Drop your left hand underneath your opponent's arms and then shoot your hand out so that it pushes the shoulder.

3

Pull your opponent in with your left arm while punching with your right hand.

4

Apply an arm lock using your right arm.

5

Punch with your left hand.

6

Apply an arm lock with your left arm.

7

Step forward and strike your opponent's collarbone by using the knife-hand block action.

SUMMARY	
Name	Bassai Dai
Translation	Extract from a fortress (major version)
Number of Moves	43
Key Features	Mountain punches
	Grasping block
	Most common kata chosen for first dan black belt gradings

CHAPTER **FIVE** Kanku Dai

This kata should look familiar to anyone who knows the Heian kata, because it looks like it is made up of fragments from these kata. Kanku Dai is required learning for all black belts and it is a compulsory kata for second dan gradings. It is most commonly remembered for its enigmatic and unique opening move and for its dramatic double flying kick. It is also significantly longer than most Shotokan kata.

Origins

The Kanku kata is thought to have been created by Kong Su Kung, the Chinese military attaché to the Okinawan court, or possibly by his student Sakugawa. The Okinawan pronunciation of Kong Su Kung is "Kushanku," and this is the name used for this kata by many styles of karate, including Wado-ryu. The Japanese pronunciation of the same characters is "Kosokun" and this name is used in Shito-ryu karate. Kosokun translates into English as "diplomat."

At some point, Kushanku was renamed to Kanku, which means "view the sky," a name presumably inspired by the first move of the kata. Just like Bassai, there are two versions of Kanku in Shotokan: Kanku Dai and Kanku Sho.

Kanku Dai written in kanji

Importance

Kanku Dai is one of the "big four" along with Bassai Dai, Empi and Jion. It is a shitei (compulsory) kata in competitions organized by the World Karate Federation (WKF), which means that you need to know this kata to make it through the opening rounds of many competitions.

Kanku Dai is the "master kata" for Shotokan karate and references many of the other Shotokan core kata. In some cases, the sequences contain subtle differences, but most are performed in exactly the same way as they are in the other kata.

KANKU DAI IN RELATION TO OTHER SHOTOKAN KATA	
Moves	*Kata Referenced*
5–9	Bassai Dai
10–15	Heian Nidan
16–17	Heian Yondan
26–31	Heian Yondan
32–35	Heian Shodan, Heian Nidan
36–37	Heian Yondan
51–53	Heian Sandan
55–57	Tekki Shodan

New Techniques

DOUBLE JUMPING KICK

Nidan Tobi-geri

When first practicing this move, try it first with just a knee lift in place of the first kick. Once you get used to the jump, try adding that first kick.

1

Start in a front stance with your left leg forward and arms crossed in front.

2

Jump up and lift your right knee, kicking to middle level. Focus on getting height rather than distance on this movement. You have to get a good jump and snap this kick, otherwise you won't have time to complete the second one.

3

As soon as your right leg is extended, strongly lift your left knee and kick to head level.

Kata Sequence

Bow. Announce the kata "Kanku Dai."

Start in ready stance.

1

Open your hands with your thumbs out and bring them together so that the right overlaps the left. Your thumbnails and your first two fingers should overlap each other so that they form a triangle.

2a

Keeping your arms straight, slowly lift up your hands. As they pass in front of your eyes, keep looking through the triangle.

2b

When your arms are pointing diagonally upward, part your hands and bring them out and down in a big circle so that they meet at a low level, striking with a right knife-hand into your left palm.

3

Step out into a back stance, facing to the left. Throw your hands up to the left, blocking at head level with the back of your left hand.

4

Pivot into a back stance, facing to the right. Throw your hands up to the right, blocking at head level with the back of your right hand.

5

Move into a natural stance by shifting your left leg. Cross your right hand over your left and, using a slow, controlled movement, make a vertical knife-hand block with your left hand.

6

Without stepping, punch using your right hand.

7

Pull your right hand back to your left shoulder and then immediately fire it forward, performing an inside block while pivoting on the spot. You should bend your knees, but your feet should simply rotate in place.

8

Straighten your hips and punch with your left hand.

9

Pull your left hand to your right shoulder and then immediately fire it forward, performing an inside block while pivoting on the spot. You should bend your knees, but your feet should simply rotate in place.

10

Shift your left foot to the center and lift your right foot to your left knee. Place both fists on your left hip.

11

Kick to the right side with a side rising kick and simultaneously strike with a right back-fist strike.

Side view

12

Step down with your right foot into a back stance with a knife-hand block.

13

Step forward with your right leg into a back stance with a knife-hand block.

14

Step forward with your left leg into a back stance with a knife-hand block.

15

Block down with your left hand, palm down. Strike with a spear-hand over the top with your right hand. Kiai.

16

Turn 180 degrees counterclockwise into a front stance. Using open hands, block to the upper level with your left hand and strike with a knife-hand to head level with your right hand.

Side view

17

Front kick to head level using your right foot.

Side view

18

Turn 180 degrees counterclockwise and perform a swastika block.

19

By shifting your weight forward, move into a front stance while blocking across your face with your open left hand. Strike to the lower level with a right-side knife-hand strike.

20

Slowly draw your weight back into a short back stance, pressing down with your left arm in a similar motion to a downward block.

Side view

21

Slide your left foot forward into a front stance. Using open hands, block to the upper level with your left hand and strike with a knife-hand to head level.

22

Front kick to head level using your right foot.

23

Turn 180 degrees counterclockwise and perform a swastika block.

24

By shifting your weight forward, move into a front stance while blocking across your face with your open left hand. Strike to the lower level with a right-side knife-hand strike.

25

Slowly draw your weight back into a short back stance, pressing down with your left arm in a similar motion to a downward block.

26

Pull your left leg up to your right knee, placing both fists on your right hip and looking to the left.

27

Kick to the left side with a side rising kick and simultaneously strike with a left back-fist strike.

28

Snap your foot back (but leave your left hand out) and step down into a front stance. Simultaneously, open your left hand and strike into it with your right elbow.

29

Lift your right foot onto your left knee. Place both fists on your left hip and look to the right.

30

Kick to the right side with a side rising kick and simultaneously strike with a right back-fist strike.

31

Snap your foot back (but leave your right hand out) and step down into a front stance. Simultaneously, open your right hand and strike into it with your left elbow.

32

Step out to the left into a back stance with a left-hand knife-hand block.

33

Step forward, with your right foot at an angle of 45 degrees, into a back stance with a right-hand knife-hand block.

34

Move your right foot across 135 degrees into a back stance with a right-hand knife-hand block.

35

Step, with your left foot at an angle of 45 degrees, into a back stance with a left-hand knife-hand block.

36

Move your left foot across into a front stance. Using open hands, block to the upper level with your left hand and strike with a knife-hand to head level.

37a

Front kick with your right leg.

37b

Snap your leg backward. Simultaneously, reach forward with your left hand in a pressing block while lifting your right fist above your head.

Side view

37c

Keep both hands moving in a circular motion so that your left fist comes to your hip and your right hand swings forward and downward to perform a back-fist strike. At the same time, step forward into a crossed-leg stance.

Side view

38

Thrust your left leg backward, but leave the weight forward so that you are in a front stance. At the same time, perform an inside block.

Side view

39

Without stepping, punch with your left hand.

40

Without stepping, punch with your right hand.

41a

Pivot counterclockwise by raising your right knee. At the same time, bring your right fist up in an uppercut motion and place your left hand open-handed on your right forearm. Jab forward and back with your punching hand.

41b

Immediately drop to the floor in a long stance.

Side view

Side view

42

Stand and pivot counterclockwise into a back stance, blocking with a low-level knife-hand block.

43

Step forward with your right leg into a back stance with a knife-hand block.

44

Turn 270 degrees counterclockwise by moving your left foot, and execute a left inside block.

45

Without stepping, reverse punch with your right hand.

46

Pivot 180 degrees into a front stance while performing an inside block with your right hand.

47

Without stepping, reverse punch with your left hand.

48

Without stepping, punch with your right hand.

49

Pull your right leg up to your left knee, placing both fists on your left hip and looking to the right.

50

Kick to your right with a side rising kick and simultaneously strike with a right back-fist strike.

51

Step down with your right foot into a back stance with a knife-hand block.

52

Block down with your left hand, palm down. Step forward into a front stance and strike with a spear-hand over the top with your right hand.

53

Bend your right arm at the elbow so your hand points up, while moving your left foot so that you rotate counterclockwise. Step through with your left foot into a horse-riding stance and perform a vertical back-fist strike with your left hand. Leave the hand out – do not snap it back.

54

Slide to the left and execute a hammer-hand strike using your left hand.

55

Pull back your left hand and elbow-strike into it with your right elbow.

56

Pull both hands to your left hip, right on top of left, and look to the right.

57

Downward block to the right with your right arm.

58a

Lift your left leg, pivoting 180 degrees on your right foot. Simultaneously, lift your left hand above your head.

58b

Stamp down with your left leg, landing in a horse-riding stance. Simultaneously, rotate your arms in a large circle, as if you were turning a big wheel, so that your left arm finishes at low level and your right arm finishes above your head.

59

Punch down to the low level with your right fist so that it finishes on the inside of your left forearm.

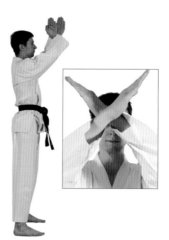

60

Pull your hands in close to your body, then instantly open your hands and shoot them up for a head-level cross-block. Simultaneously, slide your feet in so that they are hip-width apart and straighten your knees so that you stand in a natural stance.

61

Side view

Move your left foot and turn 270 degrees clockwise. As you settle into a front stance, slowly pull your hands down and close them into fists.

62a

Leap up and execute a left-leg front kick to the middle level.

62b

While still in the air, front kick with your right leg to head level. Kiai.

63

Side view

Land in a front stance and attack with a right-hand back-fist strike.

64a

Move your left leg, pivoting 180 degrees on your right foot while scooping to the low level with your right hand.

64b

Straighten your legs and lift both arms in a circular motion.

64c

Keep your arms moving in a circle until you finish in a ready stance.

Variations

The similarities with other kata like Bassai Dai and Heian Yondan are revealing: some sequences that seem identical are in fact typically performed in a subtly different way. It seems likely that these slight differences crept in over the years due to karate instructors misremembering the kata, but it is difficult to know now which was the original form and which is the newcomer.

VIEWING THE SKY (MOVE 2): SMOOTH OR ABRUPT?

Originally, this was performed as one smooth motion. Over the years, kata performers have embellished it so that it starts smoothly, but then the hands-breaking-apart move is done abruptly before the smooth motion is resumed. Another variation is that the last few inches of the move are also done abruptly. Performers of the Shito-ryu version of this kata, which they call Kushanku Dai, still do this move in one smooth motion.

VERTICAL KNIFE-HAND (MOVE 5): LIKE BASSAI?

The vertical knife-hand block move is often described as being just like in Bassai Dai, but actually it is most often performed slightly differently. The Bassai Dai version is done as two moves: the hands are brought to the hip in a "cup and saucer" position before the vertical knife-hand block. In the Kanku Dai version, it is done as one smooth motion, crossing the arms and then performing the block. The Shito-ryu version of Kanku Dai, Kushanku Dai, is done in the same way as Bassai Dai, so this might have been the original form of the move. The single smooth movement seems to be the universal way for Shotokan practitioners.

SCOOP AND THROW (MOVE 64): ONE OR TWO SCOOPS?

Most Shotokan performers do this move by scooping with the right arm and then lifting with both arms. Some performers scoop with both arms, then lift with both arms. Again, comparison with the Shito-ryu version is interesting: their Kushanku Dai is done using only one arm for the scoop and the lift.

Performance tips

This is a long kata. This means that performers often start to tire near the end. To ensure this doesn't happen, you will need to put in extra effort as the kata goes on. Use rhythm to break up the kata and make it more interesting. The slow moves act as dramatic pauses separating the different sections of the kata. Group together logically connected techniques by performing them in rapid succession, for example moves 3 and 4.

Kata Applications

ELBOW STRIKE, CHOKEHOLD APPLICATION

The first application is of moves 26 to 35 (see pages 56–58). This application uses the first back-fist strike not as an attack but as a defense, deflecting the incoming attack. The side rising kick can be effective when directed at the ribs, but in this application it is aimed at the knees, which are a more practical and effective target. When doing these kicks, the best results are achieved by dropping your body weight into the kick. Care must be taken when practicing with a partner because this technique can cause serious damage to the knee joint.

The second back-fist strike/elbow strike combination is used to apply a chokehold. You must use caution if practicing this technique with a partner because it applies pressure to the neck. Depending on how it is applied, the chokehold can compress the upper airway, damaging the larynx and leading to asphyxia, or it can compress the carotid artery that supplies blood to the brain, rapidly causing unconsciousness (as quickly as four seconds).

The back-fist strike action can be used to apply a chokehold

1

The attacker swings a punch at your head. Block with the back-fist strike action, while simultaneously performing a side kick.

2

Follow up with an elbow strike.

3

Slide past your opponent and attack the front leg with a side kick.

4

Attack your opponent's head with an elbow strike.

5

Apply a chokehold using your right arm.

ROTATING AND UPEND APPLICATION

This application is of moves 57 to 59 (see page 62). It uses the unusual rotating motion (move 59) to grab and lift the opponent. This is a very dangerous move because it can upend an opponent, dropping them on their head and possibly causing serious injury or even death. Extra caution must be used when performing this with a partner.

1

Your opponent performs a straight attack to the middle level. Deflect the attack using a downward block.

2

Grab your opponent's neck with your left hand and strike with your rear knee.

3

Stamp down, attacking the knee.

4

Grab under your opponent's left leg with your right arm. Using a rotating motion, upend your opponent.

5

Punch down to hit your opponent on the ground.

SUMMARY	
Name	Kanku Dai
Translation	View the sky (major version)
Number of Moves	64
Key Features	Jumping double kick
	Introduces the concept of going to ground
	Strong connections with other Shotokan kata.

CHAPTER **SIX** Empi

Empi has a light feeling to it with fast moves that dart in and out, attacking then escaping. This makes it a good kata for those who are light on their feet. It also contains a difficult jumping move that favors the athletic performer. It is an optional kata for brown belts and is compulsory in second dan gradings.

Origins

Empi means "flight of the swallow" (a reference to the bird). Originally, it was called Wanshu, which is believed to be the name of the Chinese emissary who brought this kata to Okinawa in the 17th century and taught it to Takahara. The kata was then passed on to Matsumura via Sakugawa.

Wanshu was renamed by Gichin Funakoshi when he brought karate to Japan. When romanized, it can be written "Enpi" or "Empi" (they are equivalent).

Empi written in kanji

Importance

Empi is one of the "big four," along with Bassai Dai, Kanku Dai and Jion. It does not have much in common with the other Shotokan kata and it contains unique moves such as the rising punch and the double-handed pressing block. Empi includes a full 360-degree jump, taking the jump learned in Heian Godan to the next level. This jump is initially difficult to perform but, with sufficient practice, can be very impressive.

New Techniques

RISING PUNCH

Age-zuki

Instead of traveling directly into its target, the rising punch is actually aimed just below the target area but then lifts up at the last moment. This is an effective move when aimed under the chin, resulting in the chin being lifted and the head being knocked back.

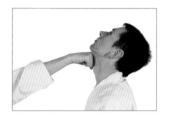

The rising punch hits under the chin, knocking the head back

1

Start in a front stance.

2

Punch to a target just below head height.

3

Just as the punch is completing and you have rotated your fist, lift your fist to complete a rising punch.

DOUBLE-HANDED PRESSING BLOCK

Morote Osae Uke

The double-handed pressing block uses the palm heel part of the hand as its contact point. The move is typically used to apply an arm lock. One hand presses down on the wrist, while the other lifts at the elbow causing a painful hyperextension of the elbow joint.

A double-handed pressing block.

1

Start in a natural stance.

2

Lift your right hand with the open palm facing down. Drop your left hand with the open palm facing up.

3

Step forward with your left leg into a front stance while pressing down with your right hand and lifting up with your left hand.

IMMOVABLE STANCE

Fudo-dachi

The immovable stance is also often called the "sochin" stance because it is so prominent in the kata Sochin. It is halfway between being a horse-riding stance and a front stance. In an immovable stance, your weight should be further forward than in a horse-riding stance but slightly further back than in a front stance. Your feet should point further forward than in a horse-riding stance, where they point to the side, but your front foot should not point straight forward as it would in a front stance.

1

Start in a horse-riding stance.

2

Push your weight forward toward one leg and turn your front foot 45 degrees in that direction.

Kata Sequence

Bow. Announce the kata "Empi."

Start by moving your feet together. Bring your hands to your left hip, with your right fist touching your open left hand.

1

Drop down into a kneeling position to the left by stepping out one shoulder-width with your left leg and bending both knees. At the same time, bring your left fist to your stomach, and with your right arm block down to the low level to the side of your right thigh.

2

Stand up in a natural stance and bring both fists to your left hip.

3

Step out to the right and perform a downward block with your right arm. Do not use a preparation for this move: your right hand should go directly downward.

4

Shift into a horse-riding stance by rotating your hips and pulling your weight back to the center. At the same time, hook punch with your left arm. This should be a fast and direct movement without any preparation.

5

Step forward with your left foot into a front stance and perform a downward block with your left arm.

6

Without stepping, perform a rising punch with your right arm.

7

Open your right hand.

8a

Launch forward by lifting your right knee.

8b

Land in a crossed-leg stance. Block across your face with your right hand and punch to the lower level with your left hand.

9

Step back with your left foot into a front stance and block behind you with your right arm. Lean away from the block but look toward it.

10

Straighten up and perform a downward block in the opposite direction with your left arm.

11

Without stepping, perform a rising punch with your right arm.

12

Open your right hand.

13a

Launch forward by lifting your right knee.

13b

Land in a crossed-leg stance. Block across your face with your right hand and punch to the lower level with your left hand.

14

Step back with your left foot into a front stance and downward block behind you with your right arm. Lean away from the block but look toward it.

15

Straighten up and block in the opposite direction with your left arm.

16a

Slowly, lift your left knee and your left arm and move them in an arc together. Keep your elbow at 90 degrees and your hand open and facing toward you throughout.

16b

Keep moving in an arc and put your foot down, settling into a horse-riding stance.

17

Execute a forearm strike int your left palm while lifting your right foot behind your left knee. Kiai.

18

Cross your left hand under your right armpit and step back down into a horse-riding stance. Slowly, perform a vertical knife-hand block with your left arm.

19

Punch with your right fist.

20

Punch with your left fist.

21

Step to the left into a front stance. Downward block with your left arm.

22

Perform a rising punch with your right arm.

23

Step forward into a back stance. Execute a knife-hand block with your right arm.

24

Switch feet by quickly moving your right foot back to your left foot, then stepping forward into a back stance with your left foot. Perform a knife-hand block with your left arm.

25

Staying in a back stance reverse punch on the spot.

26

Step forward into a back stance. Perform a knife-hand block with your right arm.

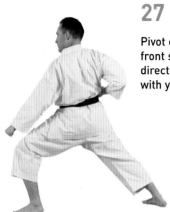

27

Pivot counterclockwise into a front stance, facing the other direction. Downward block with your left arm.

28

Without stepping, execute a rising punch with your right arm.

29

Open your right hand.

30a

Launch forward by lifting your right knee.

30b

Land in a crossed-leg stance. Block across your face with your right hand and punch to the lower level with your left hand.

31

Step back with your left foot into a front stance and block behind you with your right arm. Lean away from the block, but look toward it.

32

Straighten up and block in the opposite direction with your left arm.

33

Open and slowly lift your right hand, performing a rising pressing block. Direct this move at a 45-degree angle.

34

Move your left foot in to your center and then step out to your right with your right foot. At the same time, drop your right hand and lift your left. Then, at an increasingly slow pace, perform a double-handed pressing block, pushing up with a right-hand palm heel block and pushing down with your left.

35

Step forward into a front stance. At the same time, rotate your hands and perform a double-handed pressing block, pushing down with a right-hand palm heel block and pushing up with your left. These moves should start quickly and decelerate throughout the motion.

36

Step forward into a front stance. At the same time, rotate your hands and perform a double-handed pressing block, pushing down with a left-hand palm heel block and pushing up with your right. These moves should start quickly and decelerate throughout the motion.

37

Slide forward with your right leg into a back stance. Block down with your right arm.

38

Slide forward with your right leg into an immovable stance. Leaning forward slightly, grab at head level with your left hand and at lower level with your right hand.

39a

By lifting your right leg, jump and rotate 360 degrees counterclockwise. Cross your arms in the knife-hand block preparation position. Kiai.

39b

Land in a back stance. Perform a knife-hand block with your right hand.

40

Step back into a back stance. Perform a knife-hand block with your left hand.

Finish by slowly moving your left foot back to meet your right and by bringing your hands to your left hip, right fist touching your open left hand.

Variations

MOVE 2: STRAIGHT BACK OR CIRCULAR BLOCK?

Most commonly, the right hand is pulled directly to the left hip. In another variation of this move, the right arm moves in an arc, sweeping across the face before dropping to the left hip. In yet another variation of this move, the hand is moved slowly and smoothly rather than abruptly.

MOVES 7, 12, 29: WITH FRILLS OR PLAIN VANILLA?

The most common form of this move is simply to open the hand. Another way is to twist the hand in a little clockwise circle.

MOVE 18: FAST OR SLOW?

Most people perform the vertical knife-hand block as a slow, steady move. To do it this way, complete the preparation for the move quickly, moving your left hand under your armpit while stepping down into horse-riding stance. Once in stance, slow the technique down, executing the vertical knife-hand block slowly and steadily. An alternative method is to perform this move rapidly all the way through, so that it completes as your foot touches the ground.

Performance Tips

The start of the kata contains many quick moves, while the second half includes many slow ones. Try to contrast these quick and slow movements by making the quick ones as abrupt as possible, and the slow ones as smooth and steady as possible.

The rising punch and the subsequent two moves (moves 6 to 9, 11 to 14 and 28 to 31) should be performed in rapid succession so that they form one combination. Other moves that work well in combination are moves 23 to 24 and 37 to 39.

To make the jump look good, tuck your legs in as tightly as you can at the peak of the jump. By doing this, it'll look like a high jump, even if you aren't actually getting that far off the ground. In this way, the jump is no different from the one in Heian Godan.

Kata Applications

GRAB AND HOIST

This application is of moves 36 to 39 (see pages 81–82). It interprets the jumping move, which has earned Empi the nickname "dumping form," as a throw. You must use caution if practicing this move with a partner because it drops your opponent from a great height. Unless done very carefully, there is a risk of serious injury or death if your opponent lands on their head.

1

The attacker starts grappling by grabbing your jacket with both hands.

2

Apply an arm lock on your opponent's right arm by pressing down on the wrist with your left hand and pressing up on the elbow with your right hand.

3

Slide in and attack to the groin with a downward block motion.

4

Grab your opponent at throat level using your left hand while your right goes under your opponent's left leg.

5

Lift your opponent.

6

Dump your opponent on the ground.

GRAPPLE AND UNBALANCE

This is an application of moves 16 to 20 (see page 78). These moves use a horse-riding stance, which indicates very close-range fighting, the only range at which this stance is effective. The application uses the foot movements to disrupt your opponent's stance, something that the low stances of Shotokan karate are very effective at doing. You must use caution if practicing the forearm strike technique (step 3, below) with a partner. This technique braces your opponent's forearm while striking the elbow, which can cause hyperextension of the joint.

Move 17 from Empi causes a hyper-extension of the elbow.

1

The attacker tries grappling you with both hands.

2

Lift your left foot and step down on the back of your opponent's right knee to disrupt their stance. At the same time, break your opponent's grip by moving your arm around in an arc.

3

With your left arm touching the inside of your opponent's left arm, attack the elbow with a right forearm strike. At the same time, lift your right foot and move your weight onto your left foot.

4

Step down with your right foot so that your knee hits the inside of your opponent's thigh, disrupting their stance. You should land in a horse-riding stance so that you are very close to your opponent.

5

Using your left hand, further unbalance your opponent by pushing them back.

6

Double punch to your opponent's stomach to further unbalance them.

SUMMARY	
Name	Empi
Translation	Flight of the swallow
Number of Moves	40
Key Features	Light, fast-flowing combinations
	Rising punch combination
	Full 360-degree jumping move

CHAPTER **SEVEN** Jion

Jion is a strong, down-to-earth kata composed of big stepping techniques that will be familiar to the Shotokan practitioner. It is an optional kata for brown belts and is compulsory in second dan gradings.

Origins

Most commonly, Jion is literally translated as "temple sound." However, nobody can say definitively what the actual kanji are for Jion. There are other kanji that are pronounced the same, but which mean "temple of mercy" or "temple of love."

Jion or "temple sound," written in kanji

Importance

Jion is one of the "big four" Shotokan kata along with Bassai Dai, Kanku Dai and Empi. It is a shitei (compulsory) kata in World Karate Federation (WKF) competitions, which means that you need to know this kata to make it through the opening rounds of many competitions.

There are two other kata in the Shotokan system that share many similarities with Jion: Jitte and Ji'in. They all have the same starting position and contain a sequence of three palm-heel strikes (although in Ji'in they have a slightly different trajectory so that they hit as knife-hand strikes). Ji'in also shares Jion's angled wedge blocks that are followed up with front kicks and punches (moves 2 to 11).

Jion follows a pattern similar to one of Shotokan's most simple kata, Heian Shodan. This, combined with its familiar Shotokan techniques, makes Jion a good kata to learn after Bassai Dai.

New Techniques

PALM-HEEL STRIKE

Teisho uchi

The palm-heel is an often-overlooked strike. The closed-fisted punch is the attack of choice for the average karate practitioner, and in sports karate it is almost exclusively the only hand technique that is used (or allowed by the rules). But punching with a closed fist has a big disadvantage in a real fighting situation: if you hit anything hard, like a jawbone or a skull, you risk injuring your hand. The Okinawan karate masters knew this and used rather brutal conditioning exercises to toughen up their knuckles. Veterans of the no-holds-barred contest, Ultimate Fighting Championship, also know this and, when the contest was bare-fisted, often used the palm-heel strike in preference to a punch. This is because the palm heel is naturally tough, even without any conditioning, and can be used to hit as powerfully as a punch but without the risk of self-injury.

Palm-heel strike uses the fleshy part of the hand at the base of the palm.

1

Start in a front stance with your left leg forward.

2

Slide your right foot forward, keeping your right hip back as far as possible.

3

Push your right hip forward and step with your right foot so that you finish in a horse-riding stance. Use the hip movement to fire your right hand forward. Open your hand and pull the fingers back so that you attack with the base of the palm. Be sure not to let your elbow swing out – your elbow should be behind your hand, driving it forward.

FALLING STRIKE

Uchi otoshi

This is a hammer-hand strike that uses the bottom of the fist to make contact. In this way, the falling strike is similar to the hammer-hand strikes in Heian Shodan and Heian Sandan but, instead of traveling in an arc, the falling strike drops down in a straight line. In Jion, this move is used in combination with a stamping action.

1 Start in a front stance with your left leg forward.

2 Lift your right arm and right knee.

3 Stamp down with your right foot, while dropping your right fist.

Kata Sequence

Bow. Announce the kata "Jion."

Start by moving your feet together. Raise your arms with your elbows bent at 90 degrees. Clasp your right fist in your left hand.

1

Step back with your left leg into a front stance. Inside block with your right arm and downward block with your left arm.

2

Step forward at 45 degrees into a front stance. At the same time, cross your arms, left in front of right, and then uncross your arms into a wedge block. This move starts quickly but proceeds with increasing tension and decreasing pace.

3

Front kick using your right leg to the middle level. Your arms should remain in the wedge block position.

4

While landing, punch with your right fist to the middle level.

5

Left punch to the middle level.

6

Right punch to the middle level.

7

Pull your front foot in to meet the left and cross your arms, right in front of left. Step forward into a front stance and open your arms in a wedge block. This move starts quickly but proceeds with increasing tension and decreasing pace.

8

Front kick using your left leg to the middle level. Your arms should remain in the wedge block position.

9

While landing, punch with your left fist to the middle level.

10

Right punch to the middle level.

11

Left punch to the middle level.

12

Move your left foot across 45 degrees and perform a rising block using your left arm.

13

Without stepping, punch with your right hand.

14

Step forward with a right-arm rising block.

15

Without stepping, punch with your left hand.

16

Step forward with a rising block using your left arm.

17

Perform a stepping punch with your right fist to the middle level. Kiai.

18

By moving your left leg, rotate counterclockwise 270 degrees and perform a swastika block.

19a

Open your left hand and reach forward while bringing your right fist to your right hip.

19b

Slide to the left and hook punch with your right fist.

Side view

20

Pivot and perform a swastika block to the right.

21a

Open your right hand and reach forward while bringing your left fist to your right hip.

21b

Slide to the right and hook punch with your left fist.

Side view

22

Step to the left. Downward block with your left arm.

Side view

23

Step forward into a horse-riding stance and attack using a right-hand palm-heel strike.

24

Step forward into a horse-riding stance and attack with a left-hand palm-heel strike.

25

Step forward into a horse-riding stance and attack with a right-hand palm-heel strike.

26

By moving your left leg, rotate counterclockwise 270 degrees and perform a swastika block.

27

Perform a double-handed block to head level while moving your right foot up to your left and straightening your legs.

28

Step to the right with your right leg and perform a swastika block.

29

Perform a double-handed block to head level while moving your left foot up to your right and straightening your legs.

30

Slowly cross your arms in front of you and then straighten them out to the side, diagonally down and away from your body.

31a

Raise your right knee and bring your fists to your hips.

31b

Lunge forward, landing in a crossed-leg stance, and perform a low-level cross block.

32

Immediately, thrust your left leg back. At the same time, abruptly bring your arms away from each other so that they straighten and point diagonally down and away from your body.

33

Step forward. Cross your arms and open them to perform two inside blocks, one with each arm.

34

Step forward and cross block to head level with your left hand on the inside.

35a

Back-fist attack with your right fist and pull your left arm back to your head as if in a rising block position.

35b

Straighten and reach with your left arm. Bring your right hand up to the right side of your head to perform an upper-level sweeping block. Perform a back-fist strike with your right hand and simultaneously bend your left arm, bringing your left hand under your right elbow.

36

Turn 270 degrees counterclockwise by moving your left foot. Inside block with your left hand.

37

Perform a stepping punch with your right hand.

38

Move your right foot so that you turn 180 degrees. Inside block with your right hand.

39

Perform a stepping punch with your left hand.

40

Step to the left. Downwar block with your left arm.

Side view

41

Lift your right knee and arm. Stamp down into a horse-riding stance while attacking with a falling strike.

42

Lift your left knee and arm. Stamp down into a horse-riding stance while attacking with a falling strike.

43

Lift your right knee and arm. Stamp down into a horse-riding stance while attacking with a falling strike.

44a

Slowly rotate 180 degrees by moving your left foot alongside your right foot. At the same time, look over your left shoulder and cross your arms with the right open hand coming over your head.

44b

Step out with your left foot into a horse-riding stance while slowly punching to the left and bringing your right fist to your chest.

45a

Slowly, look over your right shoulder and bring your left hand over your head. Your right fist remains on your chest.

45b

Slide to the right while punching to the right and pulling your left fist to your chest. Kiai.

Finish by bringing your right foot to your left and returning your hands to the start position with your right fist in your left hand.

Variations

MOVE 44: SHOOT FROM THE HIP?

A common way to perform this move is to leave the left fist on the hip and punch directly out from there. This means that the attack will follow a straight line, hitting with the knuckles. If you cross your arms first, it will move in more of an arc, making contact like a hammer-hand strike.

Performance tips

In many ways, Jion is very similar to the Heian kata in terms of the moves it includes and the general pattern it follows. This means that extra effort must be made to bring this kata to life. If you just plod through Jion, it will look like "just another Heian kata."

Many of the techniques are typical large-scale Shotokan "basic" techniques. These only look good if done with long, low stances and performed with all your strength.

Adjust the timing of the different combinations or Jion will appear dull and monotonous. Perform combination moves with only brief pauses between them but a slightly longer pause afterward. Moves that should be done this way are the rising block/punch combinations (moves 12 to 13, 14 to 15 and 16 to 17). The timing for the punch combinations at the beginning of the kata (moves 4 to 6 and 9 to 11) should be punch, pause, double punch. The triple palm-heel strike and falling strike combinations (moves 23 to 25 and 41 to 43) are commonly performed with a smaller pause between the last two techniques than between the first two so that the rhythm is one, pause, one-two.

Kata Applications

CHOKEHOLD

This application is of moves 1 to 3 (see page 94). It uses the wedge block as a chokehold. Judo practitioners call this hold a gi-choke, because it involves grabbing the opponent's gi (uniform). You must use caution if practicing this technique with a partner because it applies pressure to the neck. Depending on how it is held, the technique can compress the upper airway, which can damage the larynx and lead to asphyxia, or it can compress the carotid artery, which supplies blood to the brain, rapidly causing unconsciousness (as quickly as four seconds).

The wedge block can be used to apply a chokehold.

1

The attacker attacks with a throat grab.

2

Break the grab by stepping back and dropping your left arm down on to your opponent's right, while lifting your right arm to the right.

3

Step forward and grab your opponent in a neck throttle using a wedge block. Use the step to disrupt your opponent's stance.

4

Perform a knee strike to the groin or stomach.

5

Step down behind your opponent's leg and trap it while pushing forward with your right fist.

NECK CRANK

The next application is of moves 18 to 21a. It demonstrates the dual purpose of the swastika block, both as a simultaneous blocking and attacking move and as a headlock technique. This neck lock is often called a neck crank or cervical lock. It is a very dangerous technique that pulls the neck beyond its natural range of motion. You must use extreme caution if practicing this technique with a partner because it can cause severe ligament damage, spinal cord injury or death.

1

The opponent attacks from the side with a head punch. Duck under the punch and grab the opponent's arm with your right arm while stepping in with your left leg and attacking to the groin with a left-arm downward block.

2

Slide in close and punch with your right arm.

3

Use the swastika position to hook your opponent's neck with your left arm while pulling on the arm with your right.

4

Use your elbow to drop your opponent down on to the ground.

SUMMARY	
Name	Jion
Translation	Temple sound
Number of Moves	45
Key Features	Strong, grounded kata using large-scale techniques
	Palm-heel strikes
	Falling strikes

CHAPTER **EIGHT** Hangetsu

This kata is characterized by strong, tense and slow movements, with the hands and feet moving in circular motions. It is an optional kata for brown belts and is compulsory in second dan gradings, though it is rarely asked for by grading examiners.

Origins

Hangetsu is thought to have its roots in Chinese boxing styles from the Fujian Province. In Okinawa, this kata was called Seisan (or Seishan), which simply means "13." It is still referred to by this name by practitioners of other styles of karate including Shito-ryu and Wado-ryu. There are many theories as to the significance of the number 13 – the number of steps, the number of unique techniques, the number of breaths – but there's no way of knowing, especially as the kata has changed over the years.

It was renamed "Hangetsu" by Gichin Funakoshi as part of his effort to make karate more Japanese. Hangetsu, which means "half moon," supposedly got its name from its characteristic semicircular foot and hand movements. When the word Hangetsu is pronounced in isolation, the final "u" sound is omitted as if it were just "Hangets." In fact, the "u" sound is vocalized, but is cut very short, so you can't hear it unless you listen very carefully.

Hangetsu, or "half moon," written in kanji

It is often stated that Hangetsu originates from the Naha-te school of karate, but it would be more correct to say that Shotokan's Hangetsu and Naha-te's Seisan have a common ancestor.

Importance

Hangetsu is quite unlike any of the other kata in the Shotokan system and seems out of place. It bears more resemblance to Goju-ryu kata, such as Sanchin, which are performed slowly with strong breathing. It lacks the dynamic lunging attacks that most Shotokan practitioners are used to and contains no flashy kicks or jumps. Consequently, it is rarely chosen as a competition or grading kata. The ironic thing is that the Shotokan version is the only one to have those characteristics. The Seisan kata from other styles follow the same general pattern as Hangetsu but include plenty of kicks and fast, flashy combinations.

New Techniques

HALF-MOON STANCE

Hangetsu Dachi

Make a half-moon stance by standing with your feet one shoulder-width apart. Step forward two shoulder-lengths. Rotate your front leg thigh so that your knee and toes point in at about 45 degrees.

Half-moon stance

Half-moon stance, side view

The half-moon is taught as an "inside tension" stance by many instructors, meaning that you should actively be pulling your legs in with tense muscles. This can put unhealthy and unnecessary stresses on the joints and can cause knee pain. It is better to think of it as an "inside rotation" stance. Just ensure that your knee points in the same direction as your toes.

ONE-KNUCKLE FIST

Ippon Ken

To form a one-knuckle fist, make a fist as normal, but then push the knuckle of your first finger forward slightly and brace it with your thumb.

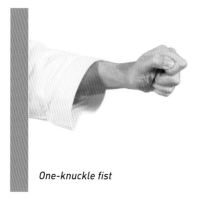

One-knuckle fist

CAT STANCE

Nekko-ashi-dachi

Cat stance (literally "cat foot stance") puts all the weight on your rear leg, leaving your front leg just lightly touching the ground. Be careful not to let your rear foot point out to the side. Instead, it should be rotated more to the front. In most styles of karate it points out at 45 degrees. The Shotokan way of doing the cat stance is to have your rear foot pointing even further forward, which will mean that your rear knee will be tucked in.

Cat stance

Kata Sequence

Bow. Announce the kata "Hangetsu."

Start in a ready stance.

1

Slowly, step forward with your left foot into a half-moon stance. At the same time, cross your left arm under your right, keeping both fists closed, and then open your arms to perform a left inside block.

2

Slowly, reverse punch.

3

Slowly, step forward with your right foot into a half-moon stance. At the same time, cross your right arm under your left, keeping both fists closed, and then open your arms to perform a right inside block.

4

Slowly, reverse punch.

5

Slowly, step forward with your left foot into a half-moon stance. At the same time, cross your left arm under your right, keeping both fists closed, and then open your arms to perform a left inside block.

6

Slowly, reverse punch.

7

Leave your right arm out and slowly push your left fist until it is alongside it. At the same time, change your fists into one-knuckle fists.

8

Slowly, bring both arms back to your chest.

9

Slowly, punch forward using both one-knuckle fists, one shoulder-width apart.

10

Slowly open your hands and cross your arms in front of your face. Open your arms out so that your hands are at the sides of your head, palms facing inward. This is known as yama gamai, mountain posture.

11

Slowly using a circular motion, cross your arms in front of you. Continue this circular motion so that your hands move down to your sides with the palms facing inward.

Side view

12

Move your right foot forward and pivot 180 degrees counterclockwise on your left foot, finishing in a half-moon stance. At the same time, perform an open-handed inside block with your right hand and an open-handed downward block with your left hand.

Side view

13

Slowly, rotate your right palm so it faces away from you, performing a grasping block. When you do this, pull your right arm back slightly.

14

Step forward with your right foot into a half-moon stance. At the same time, perform an open-handed inside block with your left hand and an open-handed downward block with your right hand.

15

Slowly, rotate your left palm so it faces away from you, performing a grasping block. When you do this, pull your left arm back slightly.

16

Step forward with your left foot into a half-moon stance. At the same time, perform an open-handed inside block with your right hand and an open-handed downward block with your left hand.

17

Slowly, rotate your right palm so it faces away from you, performing a grasping block. When you do this, pull your right arm back slightly.

18

Step to the right into a half-moon stance, slightly sliding forward at the end of the step. Inside block with your right hand.

19

Without stepping, reverse punch with your left hand.

20

Without stepping, punch with your right hand.

21

Move your left foot so that you turn 180 degrees and then slide forward, finishing in a half-moon stance. Inside block with your left hand.

22

Without stepping, reverse punch with your right hand.

23

Without stepping, punch with your left hand.

24

Step to the right into a half-moon stance, slightly sliding forward at the end of the step. Inside block with your right hand.

25

Without stepping, reverse punch with your left hand.

26

Without stepping, punch with your right hand.

27a

Lift your left foot up slowly and move it around in an arc. Your left arm should lift at the same time.

27b

Put your foot down, finishing in a back stance with your left arm in an inside block position.

Side view

28

Slowly step with your right foot so that you put your toes down just in front of your left foot.

29

Front kick with your left leg.

30

Step down into a half-moon stance. Downward block with your left arm.

31

Reverse punch with your right hand.

32

Perform a rising block with your left arm.

33a

Lift your right foot up slowly and move it around in an arc. Your right arm should lift at the same time.

33b

Put your foot down, finishing in a back stance with your right arm in an inside block position.

34

Slowly step with your left foot so that you put your toes down just in front of your right foot.

35

Front kick with your right leg.

36

Step down into a half-moon stance. Downward block with your right arm.

37

Reverse punch with your left hand.

38

Perform a rising block with your right arm.

39a

Lift your left foot up slowly and move it around in an arc. Your left arm should lift at the same time.

39b

Put your foot down, finishing in a back stance with your left arm in an inside block position.

40

Extend your left arm with your hand open. Crescent kick with your right foot into your left hand.

41

Put your right foot back down where it came from, finishing in a half-moon stance. At the same time, punch to low level with your right hand. Kiai.

42

Slide back into a cat stance. At the same time, bring your hands to your hips in the palm-heel strike position and press down so that your wrists come together as you straighten your arms.

Move your left foot back into a ready position and finish with a bow.

Variations

There seem to be fewer variations in how Hangetsu is performed. This might be a consequence of its relative unpopularity among Shotokan performers.

MOVE 18, 21, 24: SLIDE?
Sometimes the slide is omitted.

Performance tips

Hangetsu makes extensive use of slow moves that must be performed smoothly and with increasing tension. An important aspect of performing Hangetsu is the correct use of breathing, particularly during these slow moves. There are two distinct methods that are commonly used. The first is to breathe in on the blocks and to breathe out on the punches. The other method is to breathe in and out each time a slow technique is performed, timing the inhalation to start with the initiation of the technique and the exhalation to finish with the completion of the technique.

   Whichever method you use, your breathing should not be accompanied by any noise. Throttling your breathing in an effort to produce an impressive sound does nothing to improve your technique. In fact, all you are doing is obstructing your breathing.

Kata Applications

ESCAPE FROM A BEAR HUG
This application is of moves 7 to 13 (see pages 113–14).

1

The attacker grabs you from behind in a bear hug.

2

Reach as far forward as the hold will allow, attempting to loosen the grip on your arms. Then make your hands into one-knuckle fists and pull them back so that your thumb knuckle strikes the backs of your opponent's hands. Try to spread your elbows as much as possible.

3

Drop your weight and lift your arms so that you slip out of the hold.

4

Cross your arms again and this time open them to low level. If you rotate your body slightly, you'll be able to attack to the groin level.

5

Pivot and hit your opponent's neck with a ridge-hand strike.

6

Rotate your hand and pull on the back of your opponent's neck.

7

Step into your opponent, pushing down on their neck, and trapping and lifting their arm.

CRESCENT KICK KNOCKOUT

This is an application of moves 39 to 41 (see page 119). It uses the arcing foot movement (move 39) to step down on the knee. This can cause serious injury to the knee joint so, if you practice this with a partner, be cautious. This application also uses the crescent kick to drop down on to the base of the skull. This is a pressure point, which in Chinese medicine is referred to as "Gall Bladder 20" (GB20). If delivered with sufficient force, a strike here can cause unconsciousness or, in extreme cases, death. Be careful only to use a very light touch when working with a partner and targeting this area.

1

The attacker grabs hold of your collar from behind.

2

Move your arm in an arc and turn to face your opponent, trapping their arm under your armpit. At the same time, move your left leg in an arc.

3

Put your weight down on your opponent's knee, disrupting their stance.

4

Grab your opponent by the hair or collar. Then swing your right leg up and down on to the back of the head at the base of the skull (the pressure point GB20).

5

Punch to the back of the head (again GB20) while pulling your opponent in toward you.

SUMMARY	
Name	Hangetsu
Translation	Half-moon
Number of Moves	42
Key Features	Slow, circular movements
	Techniques coordinated with breathing
	Half-moon stance
	One-knuckle fists

CHAPTER **NINE** Nijushiho

Nijushiho is a common choice of kata for grading to second dan. It is visually impressive due to the contrasting slow and quick moves.

Origins

Originally this kata was called Niseishi, which means "24." It was brought to Okinawa from South China in the 19th century, probably by Seisho Aragaki. He taught it to Kanryo Higaonna, a Naha-te practitioner, and it was from Higaonna that Kenwa Mabuni, founder of the Shito-ryu style of karate, learned Niseishi. The kata thus became part of the Shito-ryu system, but interestingly Higaonna does not seem to have taught it to his most famous student, Chojun Miyagi, the founder of Goju-ryu, and Niseishi is missing from this karate school's list of official kata.

In 20th-century Japan, Yoshitaka Funakoshi took Niseishi from the Shito-ryu system and integrated it into the Shotokan system. At this time, it became known as Nijushiho, "Nijushi" simply being the Japanese pronunciation of the Okinawan Niseishi and "ho" meaning "step" or "direction."

Nijushiho, or "24 steps," written in kanji

Importance

Because of its Naha-based roots, Nijushiho is quite unlike most of the other Shotokan kata. There are no knife-hand blocks, nor any stepping punches. It does, however, introduce techniques that are absent from most of the other Shotokan kata, which have Shuri origins. For example, the circular block at the end of Nujushiho is a move characteristic of Naha-te. It only occurs in one other Shotokan kata, Unsu, which also has Naha origins. On three occasions, Nujushiho makes use of the rising elbow strike, a technique that is absent from most other Shotokan kata, which instead use the hooking elbow strike (mawashi empi).

New Techniques

HOURGLASS STANCE

Sanchin-dachi

This stance is common in other styles of karate such as Goju-ryu and Shito-ryu, but it is rare in Shotokan, only appearing in Nijushiho and Unsu, which were imported from Shito-ryu in the early 20th century. The stance's title actually comes from the kata of the same name, which forms the core of Okinawan karate styles such as Goju-ryu and Uechi-ryu.

Hourglass stance

Hourglass, side view

RISING ELBOW STRIKE

Age-empi Uchi

The rising elbow strike is a powerful close-range technique. It can be used as a powerful body blow when accompanied by a forward motion, or alternatively as an effective head attack with the elbow connecting below the chin.

Start in front stance

Step forwards and attack with a rising elbow strike

Kata Sequence

Bow. Announce the kata "Nijushiho."

Start in ready stance.

1a

Reach forward with both hands.

1b

Step back with your right foot into a back stance, moving far enough that your left foot slides back a bit at the end. At the same time, pull back, with your right fist withdrawing to your right hip and your left open hand performing a pressing block. Start the movement quickly and then slow down as it progresses.

2

Keeping your left hand in position, slide forward, staying in back stance, and punch with your right hand under your left.

3

Slide forward into a short front stance. At the same time, drop your left hand to your right hip and then raise your elbow while retracting your right fist. Start the movement quickly and then slow down as it progresses.

4a

Move your right foot across so that you pivot 180 degrees clockwise into an hourglass stance. At the same time, open your hands and swing them in a circle so that they cross in front of your face.

4b

Keep your arms moving and pull your fists to your hips.

5

Punch to head level with your right fist and to middle level with your left fist, but with the palm side facing up.

Side view

6

Lift your right knee and perform an upper-level scissor block by bringing yo forearms together.

Side view

7

Put your right foot down into a front stance. Simultaneously, cross and then slowly open your arms to perform a wedge block.

8

Step to the left into a front stance and perform a rising block with your left arm.

9

Without stepping, attack to head level with a right-arm rising elbow strike.

10

Move your right foot slightly and shift into a horse-riding stance. Look over your right shoulder. Move your right hand to your left shoulder and perform a vertical knife-hand block with your right hand. Start the movement quickly and then slow down as it progresses.

11

Perform a side thrusting kick to the right. Pull your right hand to your hip.

12

Land in a horse-riding stance and punch to the right using your left hand.

13

Look over your left shoulder. Move your left hand to your right shoulder and perform a vertical knife-hand block with your left hand. Start the movement quickly and then slow down as it progresses.

14

Perform a side thrusting kick to the left side and pull your left hand to your hip.

15

Land in a horse-riding stance and punch to the left using your right hand.

16a

Shift your left foot in to your center. Open your right hand and drop it to perform a hooking block.

16b

Slowly, step out to the left at 45 degrees into a front stance with your right foot and push forward with both hands performing palm-heel blocks, left to head level, right to middle level.

17

Pivot 180 degrees counterclockwise into a front stance. Attack using a ridge-hand strike to head level with your right hand and, at the same time, a palm-heel strike to the lower level with your left hand.

18

Bring your right foot up alongside your left foot and swing your left hand up so that the back of it slaps under your right palm. Kiai.

19

Step back with your left foot into an immovable stance. Perform a scooping block with your left hand close to your body, and a pressing block with your right hand so your right arm finishes straight.

Side view

20

Pull your hands to your hips and punch down with both fists, left above right, with the right palm side facing up.

21

Pivot 180 degrees counterclockwise into a back stance and slowly perform a back-hand block with your left hand.

22

Step forward with your right leg into a horse-riding stance. Looking over your right shoulder, perform a rising elbow strike using your right elbow.

23

Slide to your right and cross your right arm over your left as if you were doing a downward block preparation.

24

Slide to your left, but keep looking over your right shoulder. Downward block to your right.

25

Look over your left shoulder and shift into a back stance with your left leg forward. Cross your arms and then open them to perform a back-hand block with your left hand.

26

Step forward into a horse-riding stance and slap your right elbow into your left palm.

Side view

27

Without stepping, punch down with your right fist, placing your left fist on the inside of your right elbow.

28

Step forward with your left leg into a back stance and slowly perform a back-hand block with your left hand.

29

Step forward into a horse-riding stance. Looking over your right shoulder, perform a rising elbow strike using your right elbow.

30

Slide to your right and cross your right arm over your left as if you were doing a downward block preparation.

31

Slide to your left, but keep looking over your right shoulder. Downward block to your right.

32a

Take a big step to your left so that you pivot 225 degrees counterclockwise and finish in an hourglass stance. Bring your fists to your hips.

32b

Punch to head level with your right fist and to middle level with your left fist, but with the palm side facing up.

33a

Open your hands. Bring your right hand to your left shoulder and your left hand to your right hip.

33b

Move your hands in a circle clockwise until your right is on your right hip and your left is on your left shoulder.

33c

Slowly, press forward with both hands using a palm-heel strike and step forward into an hourglass stance.

Move your right foot back into a ready position and finish with a bow.

Variations

MOVE 23, 29: SLIDE?

Sometimes the forward slide is omitted. Old JKA video footage suggests that this was the original form.

MOVES 11 AND 14: SIDE KICKS

The side thrusting kicks are believed to be recent innovations. The very oldest videos of this kata show it being performed without the side kicks and with simple knee lifts in their place. Nobody knows for sure who added the kicks, though some people have suggested that it was Tetsuhiko Asai, the former Technical Director of the JKA.

Performance Tips

Nijushiho contains a high contrast of slow, strong movements and quick, explosive movements. Make the most of these attributes when performing this kata: put all your energy into the quick moves, and make sure that the slow movements are not rushed and that you maintain focus. These are the same skills that are needed to perform a kata like Heian Godan. You can further improve the slow moves by using the more advanced timing, whereby the move starts quickly but then proceeds with increasing tension and decreasing speed.

Kata Application

THRUST KICK APPLICATION

This application is of moves 10 to 12 (see page 130). It uses the thrusting kick to target the opponent's knee. When doing this kick, the best results are achieved by dropping your body weight into the kick. But care must be taken when practicing with a partner: this technique can cause serious damage to the knee joint.

1

The attacker grabs you on your right shoulder.

2

Use a right-hand vertical knife-hand block to break the grip and grab.

3

Lift your knee and stamp down on your opponent's knee.

4

Punch.

THROAT STRIKE

This application is of moves 17 to 20 (see page 131) and it uses a spear-hand strike to target the throat (step 4, below). This type of strike is ineffective if it hits bone – in fact, you're most likely just to hurt your own fingers – but it is very dangerous when used against the softer tissue of the throat. Use extra caution when practicing this technique with a partner: a throat strike can damage the larynx and obstruct breathing. This application also uses an armbar (step 5, overleaf), which is a joint lock that hyperextends the elbow. This can be very painful and, if not done with care, could cause injury to the joint.

1

The attacker grabs you from behind. This grab could be to your hair or collar.

2

Turn and break the grip by swinging your left arm in an arc.

3

Continue rotating and hit your opponent with your right hand using a ridge-hand strike.

4

Strike your opponent's throat using the pointed fingers of your left hand.

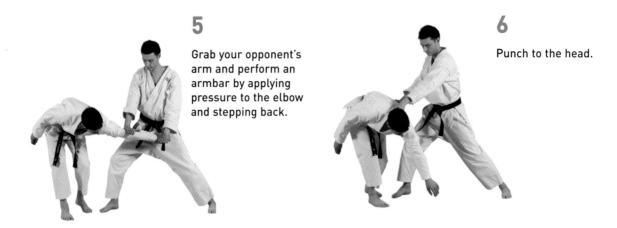

5

Grab your opponent's arm and perform an armbar by applying pressure to the elbow and stepping back.

6

Punch to the head.

SUMMARY	
Name	Nijushiho
Translation	Twenty-four steps
Number of Moves	33
Key Features	Strong, slow movements connected by light, fast combinations
	Side thrusting kick combinations
	Hourglass stance
	Double-handed circular block

CHAPTER **TEN** sparring drills

When karate was first introduced to the public in Okinawa, and then later in Japan, it did not include sparring exercises as we know them today. Prearranged sparring (yakusoku kumite) only began in the 1930s and free sparring (jiyu kumite) began some years later. At first, this was a point of controversy, particularly outside of the Tokyo universities. In *The Heart of Karate-do*, Shigeru Egami recalls disciplinary measures being taken against those who were taking part in fighting contests:

> *I heard that some karate-ka were ousted from their dojo because they had adopted sparring after having learned it in Tokyo.*

The free sparring rules were modeled on kendo, where the objective is to tag your opponent with the bamboo stick. A major influence in this was Masatoshi Nakayama, who was a keen kendo practitioner. Thus, a new form of karate was born that would become known as sports karate. So today we effectively practice two styles of fighting. The kata contain pragmatic street-fighting techniques, devastatingly effective against an opponent who isn't following any rules and is as likely to try to strangle you as hit you. Free sparring practice prepares you for a quite different scenario – one in which you are in an organized duel, one-on-one, where the first hit will win.

The sparring requirement in the second dan grading is the same as in the grading for first dan black belt (see *The Shotokan Karate Bible* for details). You will be expected to have improved the quality of your techniques and to be able to demonstrate more advanced tactics during free sparring. A basic blocking ability, a good reverse punch and a strong attitude are enough to get most people though the free sparring in their first dan grading. The advanced student needs to build up a more sophisticated repertoire, and the combinations presented here are intended to contribute to that end, rather than being fixed sequences that you will be tested on.

Fighting Posture

Kamae

The fighting posture is not a fixed, formal stance. The advanced practitioner will change his or her fighting posture depending on the circumstances. Usually, however, you will want to be in a posture that balances good offensive potential with strong defensive characteristics.

STAY ON YOUR TOES

Keep your weight slightly off your heels. Imagine that there is an ant under your heel – don't crush it. If you're on your toes, you're ready to move.

KNEES BENT, READY TO POUNCE

Keep most of your weight on your front foot and keep your knees bent. This will allow you to lunge forward or escape backward quickly. Your front foot should point forward, and your rear foot should be pointing as far forward as possible.

DON'T MAKE YOURSELF A TARGET

Turn your body side-on, so that your chest is facing to the side. Keep your head facing forward – you still need to look at your opponent.

KEEP YOUR GUARD UP

Your front arm shields your body. Keep your arm up to intercept and deflect any incoming attacks. The front arm is better at doing this than the rear arm.

BE READY TO ATTACK

Aim your fist forward to your opponent's head level and move your rear hand to stomach level. This means that you can quickly fire off an attack that moves directly toward your target.

Fighting posture

Jabbing Punch Attack

The jabbing punch is a fast attack. On its own, it is unlikely to score, but it is ideal for testing your opponent's defenses or for setting up other attacks. The jabbing attack has to be explosive. You need to be able to suddenly launch forward so that your opponent has little time to react. If you "wind up" your attack, for example by pulling your hand back before punching, you'll telegraph your attack to your opponent.

1

Start in a fighting posture.

2

Lunge forward by lifting your front leg and pushing with your rear leg. As you move, punch with your front hand.

3

As you land, pull your punching hand back and your rear leg forward so that you return to a fighting posture.

Reverse Punch Attack

The reverse punch (also known as a cross punch) is the most commonly used technique to score a point in competitions. It is ideal as a counterattacking move because it uses your rear hand, which will still be free after you have committed your front hand to deflect an attack. The key to the reverse punch is to commit your rear hip forward. If you are punching with your right hand, you need to twist your body so that your right hip and right shoulder go forward. If you fail to commit your hip, you will limit the range of the punch and most likely fail to reach your opponent.

1

Start in a fighting posture.

2

Lunge forward by lifting your front leg and pushing with your rear leg. As you move, push your rear hip forwards and attack with a reverse punch.

3

As you land, pull your punching hand back and your rear leg forward, finishing in a fighting posture.

Front Kick Footwork

Use this footwork drill to improve the speed of your front kicks when using your front leg. You can practice your front leg roundhouse kicks in the same way. This drill uses exaggeratedly low stances for training and development purposes.

1

Start in a low fighting posture with your rear knee almost touching the ground.

2

Shuffle your back foot forward toward your front foot, and lift your front leg and kick.

3

Quickly, switch your feet back to their original positions.

Roundhouse Kick Combination

The roundhouse kick is a key weapon in sparring and has an excellent chance of scoring a point in a competition. This combination maximizes your chances of bypassing your opponent's defenses with the roundhouse kick by preceding it with two punches to the head, which will tend to draw your opponent's guard up. In this combination, the roundhouse kick is targeted at stomach level, which should present none of the flexibility issues that come with a head-level kick.

1

Start by facing your opponent in a fighting posture.

2

Punch to head level using your leading hand.

3

Punch to head level using a reverse punch.

4

Kick with your back leg to stomach level using a roundhouse kick.

Foot-sweep Combination

The foot-sweep (in Japanese, ashi barai) can add a whole new dimension to your attack. Your opponent will not only have to worry about defending against head-level and stomach-level attacks, but will also have to worry about potentially unbalancing sweeps at shin height.

There are many different types of foot-sweep, but the simplest is to swing your back leg around like a roundhouse kick so that it connects with the back of your opponent's front leg. The key to a successful foot-sweep is to do it when your opponent doesn't have their weight fully on the leg you are sweeping. If your opponent is fully grounded when you sweep, with their weight heavy on the front foot, it will be as if the foot is stuck to the floor and your sweep will fail.

This combination uses head punches as a distraction and will cause your opponent to move their weight back slightly to avoid them. This will then lift some weight off the front foot, making it prone to a sweep. These punches are effectively a feint intended to create an opening, but remember that they have to be credible if they are to cause your opponent to react. A half-hearted feint will either have no effect or will simply draw a counterattack.

1

Start by facing your opponent
in a fighting posture.

2

Punch to the head level using
your leading hand.

3

Punch to the head level using
a reverse punch.

4

Use your back leg to sweep
your opponent's front leg.

5

A successful foot-sweep will
unbalance your opponent.
Follow up with a reverse
punch.

Charging Attack

Use the charging attack to rapidly close the distance between you and your opponent. If you use this combination, you must fully commit to your attack and launch forward with all your energy. If you hold back, your attack will be weakened and it will be easier for your opponent to defend and counterattack you.

1

Start by facing your opponent in a fighting posture.

2

Moving your back leg, take a step forward and punch with the opposite hand. This step can be long or short, depending on how much distance you need to cover in order to reach your opponent.

3

Take another step and punch with the other hand.

Attack and Flank

If your opponent has a strong guard and seems to block all your attacks easily, you might find this combination useful. You use your opponent's guard against them by grabbing their front hand and then launching an attack past it. If done correctly, you'll end up with your opponent facing the wrong way, and you will be effectively flanking them.

1

Start by facing your opponent in a fighting posture.

2

Use your front hand to deflect your opponent's guard, so that any attacks will be smothered.

3

Immediately, leap forward past your opponent, punching at the same time to your opponent's head.

4

As you land, pivot to face your opponent.

Rapid Counterattack

If an opponent drives you back with an attack, you can use this footwork to rapidly switch direction and come back with a strong counterattack. The key is to leave as much body weight forward as you can, enabling you to lunge forward again once you have redirected the attack. If you let your body weight go back, you will find it hard to move forward again.

1

Your opponent attacks you with a reverse punch. Block the attack and retreat slightly by moving your front foot back. Leave your body weight forward as much as possible.

2

Launch forward and attack with a stepping punch.

CHAPTER **ELEVEN** karate competitions

Gichin Funakoshi said that "there are no contests in karate." But if it were not for karate competitions, karate would not enjoy the popularity it has today. There are many different karate competitions and many different rules under which they are played. The most standardized are the rules laid out by the World Karate Federation (WKF) and these are the rules that are described here. At the time of writing, karate is not an Olympic sport. However, the WKF rules are recognized by the International Olympic Committee. If karate were ever to make it into the Olympic Games, these are the rules that would be used.

Kata Competitions

KATA CHOICES

In WKF competitions, you have to perform kata from the official list. In the first two rounds of most competitions, you perform a kata from the shitei (compulsory) list. In subsequent rounds, the kata come from the tokui (specialty) list. You cannot perform the same kata twice, which means that to get to the finals you may need to know seven kata – both of the shitei kata and five from the tokui list.

WKF RULES FOR REQUIRED KATA			
Competitors or Teams	Kata Required	Tokui	Shitei
65–128	7	5	2
33–64	6	4	2
17–32	5	3	2
9–16	4	3	1
5–8	3	3	0
4	2	2	0

WKF SHOTOKAN KATA	
Shitei (Compulsory) kata	
Jion	
Kanku Dai	
Tokui (Free selection)	
Bassai Dai	Bassai Sho
Kanku Dai	Kanku Sho
Tekki Shodan	Tekki Nidan
Tekki Sandan	Hangetsu
Jitte	Empi
Gankaku	Jion
Sochin	Nijushiho
Gojushiho Dai	Gojushiho Sho
Chinte	Unsu
Meikyo	Wankan
Ji'in	

Non-WKF competitions have different requirements. It is very common for preliminary rounds to be decided by Heian elimination. During these rounds, the referee will randomly select a Heian kata for the competitors to perform. The competitor who does it best goes through to the next round. In the final round (usually consisting of four competitors), you are usually allowed to choose your tokui kata.

DIVISIONS
Kata competitions are typically divided into male and female divisions, though it is not unheard of for them to be mixed. Some kata competitions are also divided by the grade of the competitor, usually with dan grades in one category and brown belts and below in another.

SCORING CRITERIA

WKF SCORING CRITERIA

A realistic demonstration of the kata's meaning.

Understanding of the techniques being used (bunkai).

Good timing, rhythm, speed, balance and focus of power (kime).

Correct and proper use of breathing as an aid to kime.

Correct focus of attention (chakugan) and concentration.

Correct stances (dachi), with proper tension in the legs and feet flat on the floor.

Proper tension in the abdomen (hara) and no bobbing up and down of the hips when moving.

Correct form (kihon) of the style being demonstrated.

The difficulty of the kata presented.

In team kata, synchronization without external cues is an additional scoring criteria.

Realistic Demonstration

Kata is not a dance but a demonstration of realistic fighting techniques. You should understand the meaning of the techniques you are performing.

Sharp Explosive Moves

Make the fast moves fast and the slow moves slow. This is the most important rule of kata performance. However, don't rush through the kata. This will ruin the rhythm and can result in moves being incomplete.

Breathing

Correct breathing includes a short exhalation of breath upon completion of each technique. For slow techniques, your breathing should reflect the speed of the technique. You should not constrict your breathing. Sometimes people will do this because it generates an impressive sound, but it is actually an obstruction to proper breathing and hence a mistake.

Focus of Attention

This essentially means keeping your gaze focused in the correct direction for the technique you are performing. The best way to achieve this is to have imaginary opponents that you are applying the techniques to. Ensure you keep your gaze trained on these imaginary opponents. If you allow your eyes to wander – for example, by looking at the judges, other competitors or your karate coach – it will mean you have lost focus. For each step in the kata, think about where you should be looking. When there is a change in direction, turn your head quickly to look in the new direction.

Stance and Posture

The quality of your stance is a major factor in making the kata look good. You must also maintain proper tension in your legs, with your feet flat on the floor. Keep your back straight (except of course for those few moves where you are actually required to lean, for example the mountain punches in Bassai Dai).

Kata Difficulty

The more difficult kata will, potentially at least, yield more points. Take this into account when you are choosing which kata to perform. Beware, however, of selecting a kata that is too difficult for you – you are more likely to lose points that gain them. You are better off doing a slightly easier kata perfectly than a difficult kata with mistakes.

TEAM KATA

A team kata is performed by three people in a triangular formation, all facing the same direction. In addition to the previously mentioned scoring criteria, consideration is made of how well synchronized the moves are, and how rarely external cues are used. A team kata performance would be penalized if, for example, one of the members shouted out a count to keep the moves synchronized. Remember that the performance begins from the moment you walk out on to the mat. It is quite common for the team leader to say "rei" to prompt the team to bow, to announce "hajime" to start the kata and "yame" to finish, but these are all prompts that can be penalized.

Under WKF rules, the finals of the team kata event must also include a demonstration of the meaning of the kata (bunkai), lasting five minutes or less.

Kumite Competitions

DIVISIONS

Like kata competitions, kumite competitions are usually divided into male and female categories and can also be divided by grade of competitor.

SCORING SYSTEM

Under WKF rules, the number of points you score on a successful attack depends on the nature of that attack. The scores that can be awarded for an attack are as follows:

IPPON (ONE POINT)

Head-level or middle-level punches

Strikes

Reverse punch to the stomach

Back-fist strike to the head

NIHON (TWO POINTS)

Middle-level kicks

Roundhouse kick to the lower back

Punches to the back, or back of the head, or neck

Reverse punch to the lower back

Combination hand techniques

1 *Jabbing punch to the head*

2 *Immediate follow-up with a reverse punch to the body*

Unbalancing the opponent and scoring

1 *A foot-sweep unbalances the opponent*

2 *Immediate follow-up with a reverse punch to the body*

SANBON (THREE POINTS)

Head-level kicks

Roundhouse kick to the head

Bringing the opponent to the mat followed by a scoring technique

1 *Throw*

2 *Immediate follow-up with a reverse punch to the body*

SCORING CRITERIA

In semi-contact matches, there is often confusion over exactly what counts as a scoring technique. Sometimes, a competitor will land what she or he considers to be a scoring technique, only for the referee to declare "torimasan," which means no points scored. This can lead to competitors trying to hit harder, which risks injuries as well as penalty points for insufficient control. It is therefore important to understand what the criteria are for points being awarded.

Vigorous Application

The attack must be thrown with speed and power so that it would have been effective had it not been pulled back before impact. When an attack is disallowed for not being vigorous enough, the referee will say "Yowai."

Correct Distance

Clearly, if an opponent is too far away for a technique to deliver power, you won't score a point. Equally, however, if an opponent is too close it becomes impossible to generate sufficient power and so, again, you won't score a point. When an attack is disallowed for incorrect distance, the referee will say "Maai."

Incorrect distance *Correct distance*

Good Timing

You must use the correct timing for the technique to be effective. If your opponent is moving away at the point of contact, you won't score a point. Ideally, your opponent should be moving toward your attack at the point of impact, thereby maximizing effectiveness.

Incorrect timing: opponent is moving away from the attack   *Correct timing: opponent is moving into the attack*

Angle of Attack

If the angle of your attack is such that it would have deflected off your opponent on impact, it won't score a point. An effective attack must hit its target perpendicular to its surface. That way, all the energy of the attack is directed into the target.

Incorrect angle: the attack will deflect past the target   *Correct angle: the attack is going straight into the target*

Awareness

For a technique to score a point, you must demonstrate what is known as awareness (this is usually referred to as "zanshin").

No awareness – not looking at opponent   *Scoring with awareness*

Tournament Terminology

The referee will conduct much of the competition using Japanese terms. Here are some of the more important ones.

TOURNAMENT TERMINOLOGY	
General Instructions	
Hajime	Start
Yame	Stop
Rei	Bow
Shomen ni rei	Bow to dignitaries
Shimpani ni rei	Judges and competitors bow to each other
Otagai ni rei	Competitors bow to each other
Rule Infringements	
Keikoku	Private warning, usually for minor infringement of the rules
Hansoku	Disqualification
Hansoku chui	Official warning
Jogai	The fighting area
Jogai chui	Warning for leaving the fighting area
Jogai Keikoku	Private warning for leaving the fighting area
Jogai Hansoku	Disqualification for leaving the fighting area
Shikkaku	Disqualification from the whole tournament, usually for a serious violation of the rules
Scoring	
Aiuchi	Simultaneous scoring techniques
Maai	Distance
Ukete masu	Blocked
Nukete masu	Missed
Yowai	Weak
Torimasan	No score

APPENDICES

Grading Syllabus

WHITE BELT GRADING SYLLABUS	
Basics	
Stepping punch	Oi-zuki
Rising block	Age-uke
Outside block	Soto-uke
Inside block	Uchi-uke
Front kick	Mae-geri
Kata	
Kihon Kata (Taikyoku Shodan)	
Kumite	
Five-step sparring	Gohon kumite

ORANGE BELT GRADING SYLLABUS

Basics

Stepping punch	Oi-zuki
Rising block	Age-uke
Outside block	Soto-uke
Inside block	Uchi-uke
Knife-hand block	Shuto-uke
Front kick	Mae-geri
Side thrusting kick	Yoko kekomi
Side rising kick	Yoko keage

Kata

Kihon Kata (Taikyoku Shodan)

Heian Shodan

Kumite

Five-step sparring	Gohon kumite

RED BELT GRADING SYLLABUS

Basics

Triple punch	Sanbon tsuki
Rising block, reverse punch	Age-uke, gyaku-zuki
Outside block, reverse punch	Soto-uke, gyaku-zuki
Inside block, reverse punch	Uchi-uke, gyaku-zuki
Knife-hand block	Shuto-uke
Front kick	Mae-geri
Side thrusting kick	Yoko kekomi
Side rising kick	Yoko keage

Kata

Kihon Kata (Taikyoku Shodan)

Heian Shodan

Heian Nidan

Kumite

Five-step sparring	Gohon kumite

YELLOW BELT GRADING SYLLABUS

Basics

Triple punch	Sanbon tsuki
Rising block, reverse punch, downward block	Age-uke, gyaku-zuki, gedan barai
Outside block, elbow strike	Soto-uke, empi-uchi
Inside block, reverse punch	Uchi-uke, gyaku-zuki
Knife-hand block, spear-hand strike	Shuto-uke, nukite
Consecutive front kicks	Mae ren-geri
Side thrusting kick	Yoko kekomi
Side rising kick	Yoko keage

Kata

Kihon Kata (Taikyoku Shodan)

Heian Shodan

Heian Nidan

Heian Sandan

Kumite

One-step sparring	Ippon kumite
Head-level stepping punch	Jodan oi-zuki
Stomach-level stepping punch	Chudan oi-zuki

GREEN BELT GRADING SYLLABUS

Basics

Triple punch	Sanbon tsuki
Rising block, reverse punch, downward block	Age-uke, gyaku-zuki, gedan barai
Outside block, elbow strike, back-fist strike	Soto-uke, empi-uchi, uraken-uchi
Inside block, jabbing punch, reverse punch	Uchi-uke, kizami-zuki, gyaku-zuki
Knife-hand block, jabbing front kick, spear-hand strike	Shuto-uke, kizami mae-geri, nukite
Consecutive front kicks	Mae ren-geri
Side thrusting kick	Yoko kekomi
Side rising kick	Yoko keage
Roundhouse kick	Mawashi-geri

Kata

Kihon Kata (Taikyoku Shodan)

Heian Shodan

Heian Nidan

Heian Sandan

Heian Yondan

Kumite

One-step sparring	Ippon kumite
Head-level stepping punch	Jodan oi-zuki
Stomach-level stepping punch	Chudan oi-zuki
Front kick	Mae-geri
Side thrusting kick	Yoko kekomi

PURPLE BELT GRADING SYLLABUS

Basics

Triple punch	Sanbon tsuki
Rising block, reverse punch, downward block	Age-uke, gyaku-zuki, gedan barai
Outside block, elbow strike, back-fist strike, reverse punch	Soto-uke, empi-uchi, uraken-uchi, gyaku-zuki
Inside block, jabbing punch, reverse punch	Uchi-uke, kizami-zuki, gyaku-zuki
Knife-hand block, jabbing front kick, spear-hand strike	Shuto-uke, kizami mae-geri, nukite
Consecutive front kicks	Mae ren-geri
Side thrusting kick	Yoko kekomi
Side rising kick	Yoko keage
Roundhouse kick	Mawashi-geri

Kata

Kihon Kata (Taikyoku Shodan)

Heian Shodan

Heian Nidan

Heian Sandan

Heian Yondan

Heian Godan

Kumite

One-step sparring	Ippon kumite
Head-level stepping punch	Jodan oi-zuki
Stomach-level stepping punch	Chudan oi-zuki
Front kick	Mae-geri
Side thrusting kick	Yoko kekomi

PURPLE AND WHITE BELT GRADING SYLLABUS

Basics

Triple punch	Sanbon tsuki
Rising block, reverse punch, downward block	Age-uke, gyaku-zuki, gedan barai
Outside block, elbow strike, back-fist strike, reverse punch, downward block	Soto-uke, empi-uchi, uraken-uchi, gyaku-zuki, gedan barai
Inside block, jabbing punch, reverse punch, downward block	Uchi-uke, kizami-zuki, gyaku-zuki, gedan barai
Knife-hand block, jabbing front kick, spear-hand strike	Shuto-uke, kizami mae-geri, nukite
Consecutive front kicks	Mae ren-geri
Side thrusting kick	Yoko kekomi
Side rising kick	Yoko keage
Roundhouse kick	Mawashi-geri
Back kick	Ushiro-geri

Kata

Kihon Kata (Taikyoku Shodan)

Heian Shodan

Heian Nidan

Heian Sandan

Heian Yondan

Heian Godan

Tekki Shodan

Kumite

One-step sparring	Ippon kumite
Head-level stepping punch	Jodan Oi-zuki
Stomach-level stepping punch	Chudan Oi-zuki
Front kick	Mae-geri
Side thrusting kick	Yoko kekomi
Roundhouse kick	Mawashi-geri

BROWN BELT GRADING SYLLABUS

Basics

Triple punch	Kizami-zuki, oi-zuki, gyaku-zuki
Front kick combination	Mae-geri, oi-zuki, gyaku-zuki
Side thrusting kick combination	Yoko kekomi, uraken-uchi, gyaku-zuki
Roundhouse kick combination	Mawashi-geri, uraken-uchi, gyaku-zuki
Back kick combination	Ushiro-geri, uraken-uchi, gyaku-zuki

Kata

Kihon Kata (Taikyoku Shodan)

Heian Shodan

Heian Nidan

Heian Sandan

Heian Yondan

Heian Godan

Tekki Shodan

Bassai Dai

Kumite

One-step free sparring	Jiyu ippon kumite
Head-level stepping punch	Jodan oi-zuki
Stomach-level stepping punch	Chudan oi-zuki
Front kick	Mae-geri
Side thrusting kick	Yoko kekomi
Roundhouse kick	Mawashi-geri
Back kick	Ushiro-geri

BLACK BELT GRADING SYLLABUS: 1ST KYU TO 1ST DAN

Basics

Triple punch	Kizami-zuki, oi-zuki, gyaku-zuki
Front kick combination	Mae-geri, oi-zuki, gyaku-zuki
Side thrusting kick combination	Yoko kekomi, uraken-uchi, gyaku-zuki
Roundhouse kick combination	Mawashi-geri, uraken-uchi, gyaku-zuki
Back kick combination	Ushiro-geri, uraken-uchi, gyaku-zuki
Four-kick combination	Mae-geri, yoko kekomi, mawashi-geri, ushiro-geri, uraken-uchi, gyaku-zuki
Standing kicks	Mae-geri, yoko kekomi, ushiro-geri
Shodan combination	Mae-geri, oi-zuki, gyaku-zuki, step back gedan barai, gyaki-zuki, mawashi-geri, uraken-uchi, oi-zuki

Kata

Kihon Kata (Taikyoku Shodan)

Heian Shodan

Heian Nidan

Heian Sandan

Heian Yondan

Heian Godan

Tekki Shodan

Choose one from:

Bassai Dai, Kanku Dai, Jion, Empi, Hangetsu

Kumite

One-step free sparring	Jiyu ippon kumite
Head-level stepping punch	Jodan oi-zuki
Stomach-level stepping punch	Chudan oi-zuki
Front kick	Mae-geri
Side thrusting kick	Yoko kekomi
Roundhouse kick	Mawashi-geri
Back kick	Ushiro-geri
Free sparring	Jiyu-kumite

BLACK BELT GRADING SYLLABUS: 1ST DAN TO 2ND DAN

Basics

Triple punch	Kizami-zuki, oi-zuki, gyaku-zuki
Front kick combination	Mae-geri, oi-zuki, gyaku-zuki
Side thrusting kick combination	Yoko kekomi, uraken-uchi, gyaku-zuki
Roundhouse kick combination	Mawashi-geri, uraken-uchi, gyaku-zuki
Back kick combination	Ushiro-geri, uraken-uchi, gyaku-zuki
Front kick/roundhouse kick combination	Mae-geri, Mawashi-geri, uraken-uchi, gyaku-zuki
Roundhouse kick/side thrusting kick combination	Mawashi-geri, yoko kekomi, uraken-uchi, gyaku-zuki
Roundhouse kick/reverse-back roundhouse kick combination	Mawashi-geri, ushiro ura mawashi-geri, uraken-uchi, gyaku-zuki
Front kick/back kick combination	Mae-geri, ushiro-geri, uraken-uchi, gyaku-zuki
Four-kick combination	Mae-geri, move front foot back, yoko kekomi, mawashi-geri, ushiro-geri, uraken-uchi, gyaku-zuki
Standing kicks	Mae-geri, yoko kekomi, ushiro-geri, mawashi-geri
Shodan combination	Mae-geri, oi-zuki, gyaku-zuki, step back gedan barai, gyaku-zuki, mawashi-geri, uraken-uchi, oi-zuki

Kata

Kihon Kata (Taikyoku Shodan)

Heian Shodan

Heian Nidan

Heian Sandan

Heian Yondan

Heian Godan

Tekki Shodan

Bassai Dai

Kanku Dai

Jion

Kata continued

Empi

Hangetsu

Choose one from:

Bassai Sho, Kanku Sho, Jitte, Nijushiho, Tekki Nidan

Kumite

One-step free sparring	Jiyu ippon kumite
Head-level stepping punch	Jodan oi-zuki
Stomach-level stepping punch	Chudan oi-zuki
Front kick	Mae-geri
Side thrusting kick	Yoko kekomi
Roundhouse kick	Mawashi-geri
Back kick	Ushiro-geri
Free sparring	Jiyu kumite

Advanced Shotokan Karate Kata

拔塞 **BASSAI DAI**

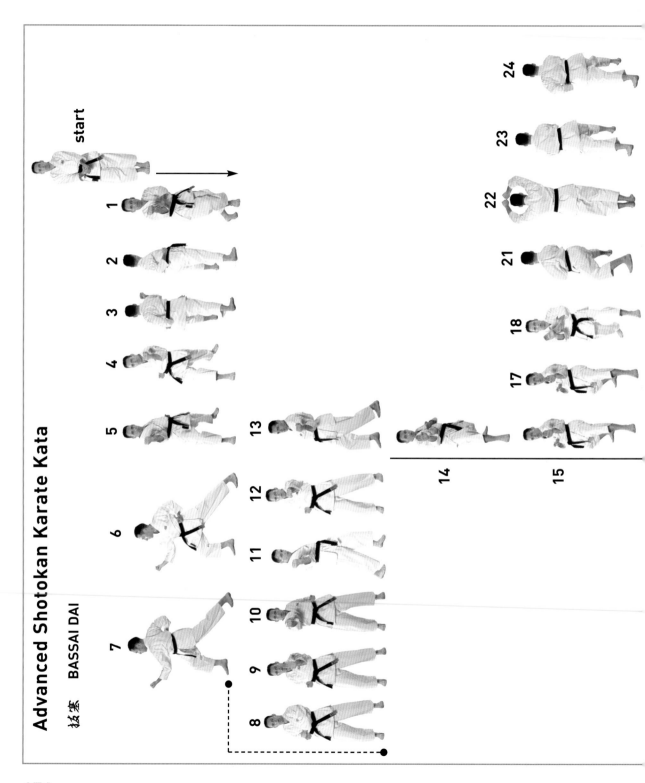

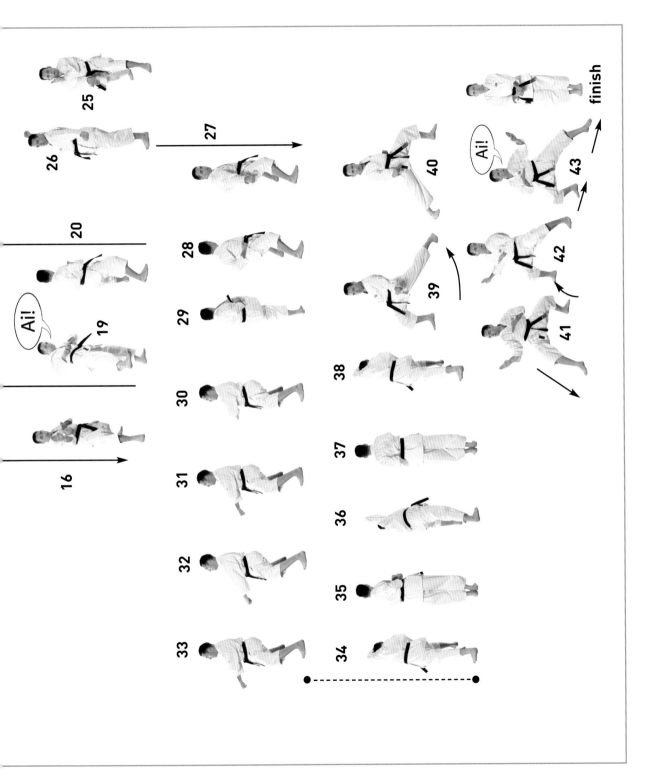

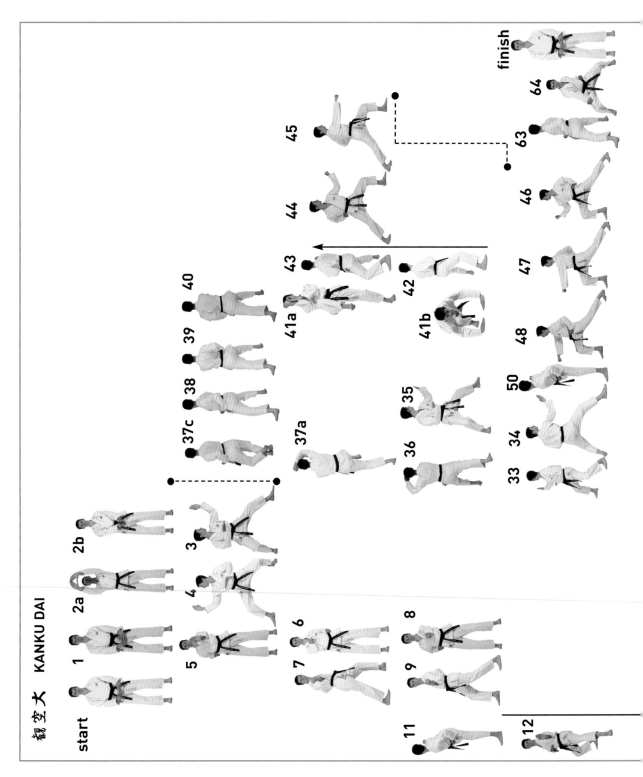

観空大 KANKU DAI

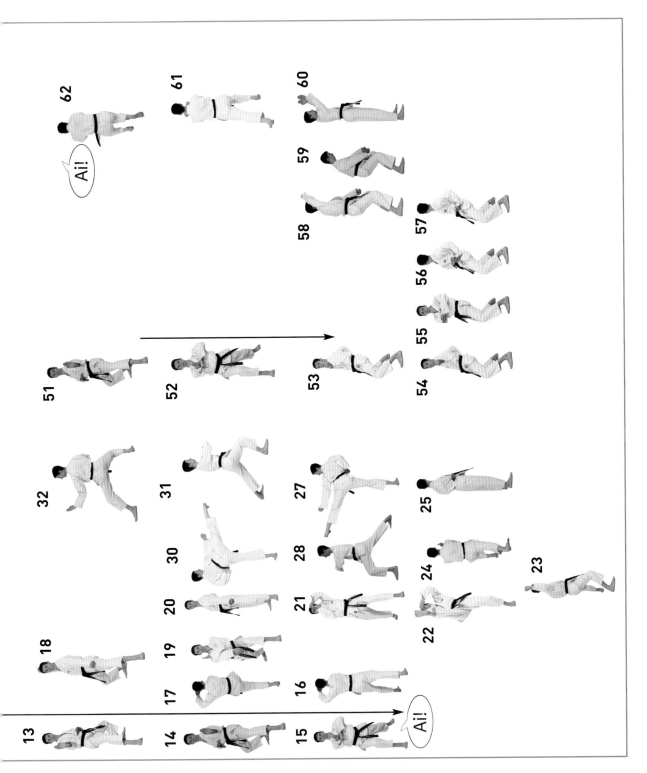

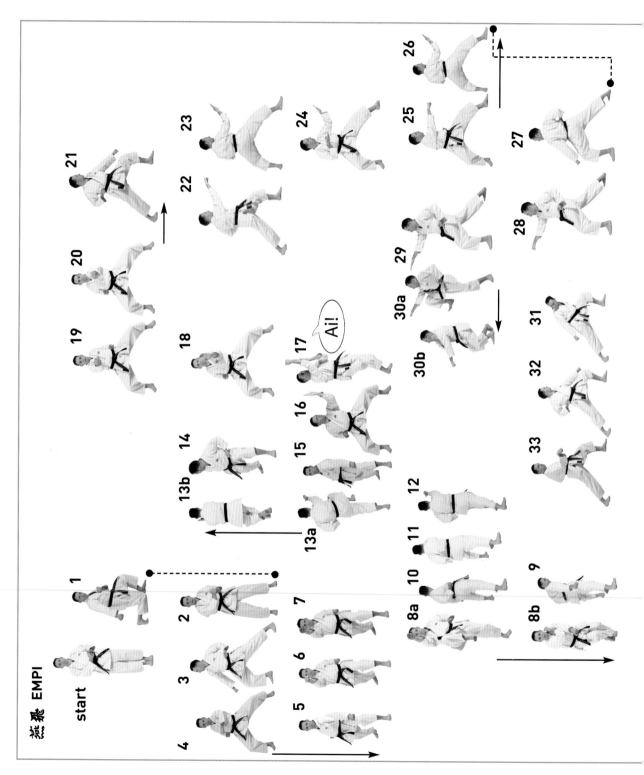

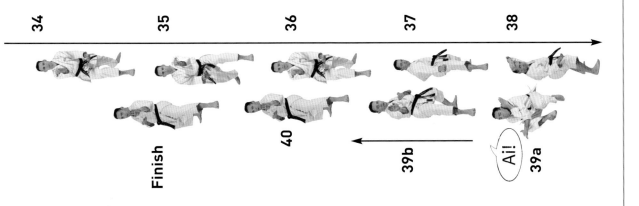

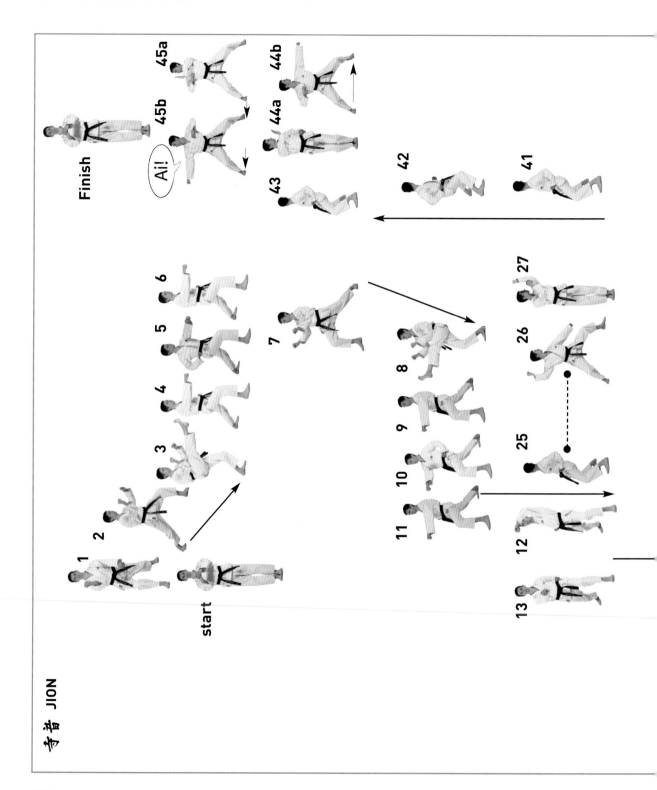

香音 JION

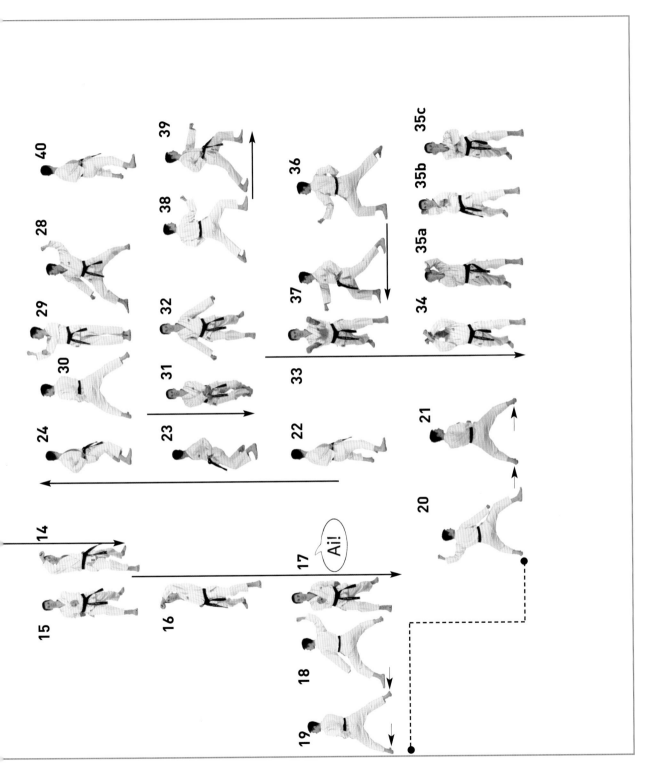

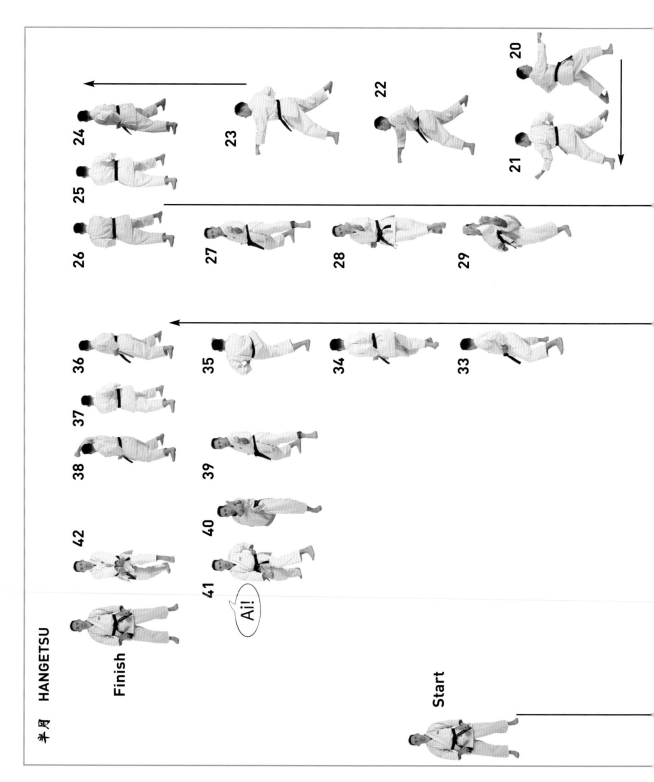

半月 HANGETSU

Finish

Ai!

Start

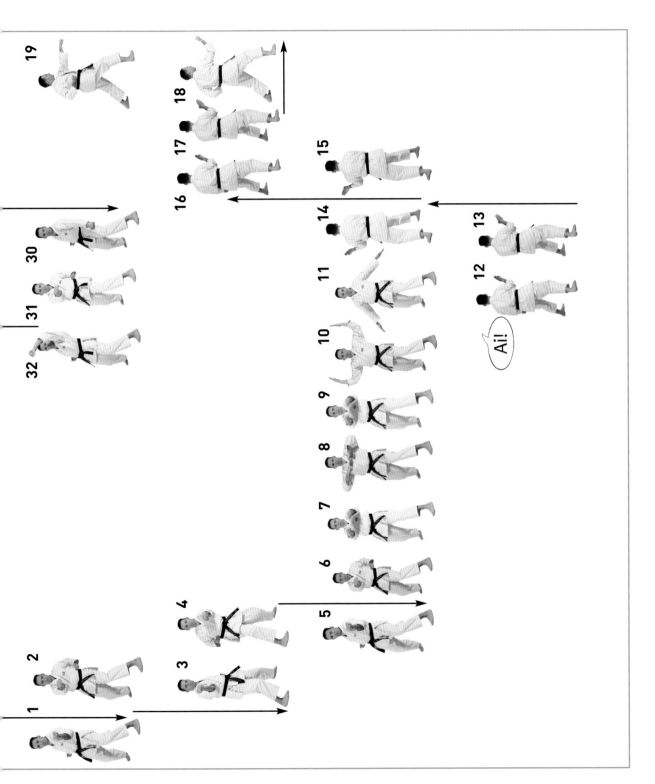

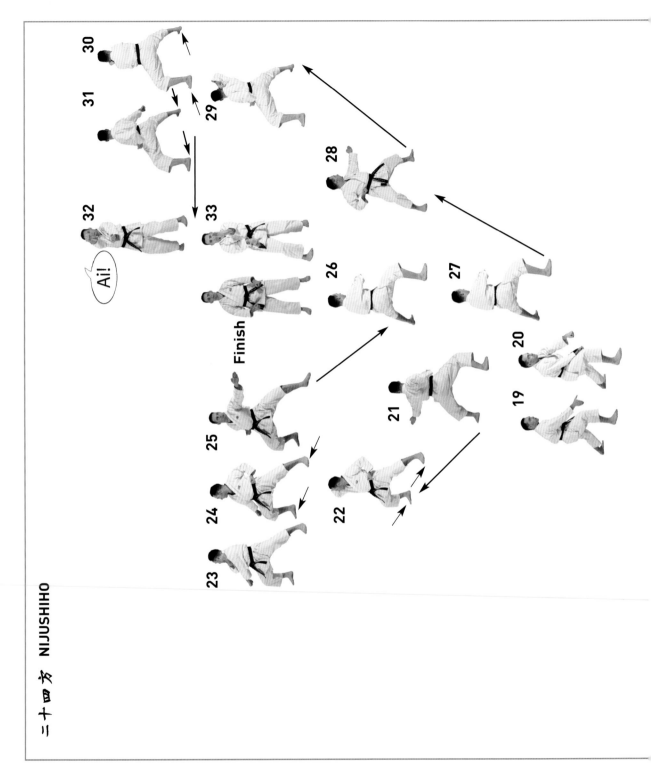

三十四方 NIJUSHIHO

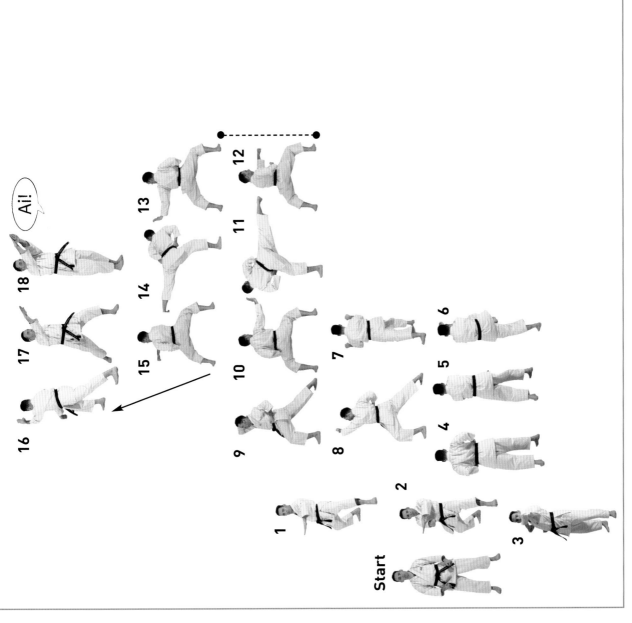

BIBLIOGRAPHY

Abernethy, I., *Bunkai Jutsu*, Neth Publishing, 2002.

Clayton, B. D., *Shotokan's Secret*, Ohara Publications Inc., 2004.

Egami, S., *The Heart of Karate-do*, Kodansha, 2000.

Fleming, I., *Goldfinger*, Cape, 1959.

Funakoshi, G., *Karate Do Kyohan*, Kodansha, 1973.

———, *Karate Do, My Way of Life*, Kodansha, 1975.

———, *Karate Do Nyumon*, Kodansha, 1988.

Haines, B. A., *Karate's History and Traditions*, Tuttle, 1995.

Lee, B., *Tao of Jeet Kune Do*, Ohara Publications Inc., 1975.

Martin, A. P., *The Shotokan Karate Bible*, Firefly Books, 2007.

Nakayama, M., *Best Karate Volume 6*, Kodansha, 1979.

———, *Best Karate Volume 7*, Kodansha, 1981.

———, *Best Karate Volume 8*, Kodansha, 1981.

———, *Best Karate Volume 10*, Kodansha, 1987.

———, *Dynamic Karate*, Kodansha, 1987.

Redmond, R., *Kata: The Folk Dances of Shotokan*, http://www.24fightingchickens.com/kata, 2006.

World Karate Federation, *Kata and Kumite Rules, Version 5.5*, http://www.karateworld.org, June 2005.

GLOSSARY

Age-empi uchi — Rising elbow strike

Age-uke — Rising block

Age-zuki — Rising punch

Bassai dai — Brown belt kata translated as "fortress extraction, major version"

Budo — Way of the warrior

Ch'uan fa — Chinese boxing (literally translated as "fist way")

Chudan — Stomach level

Dachi — Stance

Dan grade — Black belt level. Dan means "level." A first-degree black belt is called a shodan, a second-degree black belt is called nidan, and so on

Dogi — Karate uniform

Dojo — Karate training hall, literally translated as "place of the way"

Dojo kun — School code, recited in many karate schools at the beginning or end of class

Empi-uchi — Elbow strike. Empi can also be written "enpi," but it is always pronounced empi

Fudo-dachi — Immovable stance

Gedan barai — Downward block (literally translated as "lower-level sweep")

Gi — Karate uniform. Short version of dogi

Gohon kumite — Five-step sparring

Gyaku-zuki — Reverse punch

Hajime — Begin

Hangetsu-dachi — Half-moon stance

Heian — Peace. Shotokan karate contains five Heian kata: Heian Shodan, Heian Nidan, Heian Sandan, Heian Yondan and Heian Godan

Heiko-dachi — Parallel-feet stance

Heisoku-dachi — Formal attention stance (literally translated as "closed feet stance")

Ippon — In karate competitions, this means "one point"

Ippon ken — One-knuckle fist

Ippon kumite — One-step sparring

Jiyu ippon kumite — Free one-step sparring

Jiyu kumite — Free sparring

Jodan — Head level

Juji-uke — Cross block

Kagi-zuki — Hook punch

Kanji — Type of ideogram used in the Japanese writing system, literally translated as "Han characters" in reference to the Chinese Han dynasty

Kata — "Form" or "pattern." In the context of karate, this means a sequence of prearranged techniques against imaginary opponents

Keimochi — Member of the Okinawan nobility

Kempo — Literally translated as "fist way," this is the Japanese reading of the characters for ch'uan fa, Chinese boxing

Keri — Kick. When it follows another word, the sound changes to geri, as in mae-geri, mawashi-geri, and so on

Kiai	A martial shout (literally translated as "spirit unity")	**Randori**	Literally translated as "disordered engagement"
Kiba-dachi	Horse-riding stance	**Rei**	Bow
Kihon	Basic	**Samurai**	Japanese feudal warrior
Kime	Literally translated as "decision." To focus all your energy into a technique	**Sanbon kumite**	Three-step sparring
		Sanchin-dachi	Hourglass stance
Kizami-zuki	Jabbing punch	**Seiretsu**	Line up
Kokutsu-dachi	Back stance	**Sensei**	Teacher
Kosa-dachi	Crossed-leg stance	**Shiai kumite**	Tournament sparring
Kumite	Sparring	**Shitei**	Literally translated as "assigned." A shitei kata is a compulsory kata in a grading or competition
Mae-geri	Front kick		
Manji-uke	Swastika block		
Mawashi-geri	Roundhouse kick	**Shizen-tai**	Literally translated as "natural body"
Mawatte	Turn	**Shodan**	First level. A first-degree black belt is called a shodan
Mikazuki-geri	Crescent kick		
Mokuso	Meditate	**Shuri**	Historic capital of Okinawa, influential in the creation of karate
Morote-uke	Double-handed block		
Musubi-dachi	Informal attention stance (literally translated as "connected stance")	**Shuri-te**	Okinawan unarmed fighting style from the royal city of Shuri
Nagashi-uke	Passing block	**Shuto-uchi**	Knife-hand strike
Naha-te	Okinawan unarmed fighting style from the port town of Naha	**Shuto-uke**	Knife-hand block
		Soto-uke	Outside block
Nami gaeshi-geri	Returning wave kick	**Tate shuto-uke**	Vertical knife-hand block
Naore	Relax (literally translated as "put back into place")	**Teisho-uchi**	Palm-heel strike
		Tekki	Iron horse. Shotokan karate contains three Tekki kata: Tekki Shodan, Tekki Nidan and Tekki Sandan
Nekko-ashi-dachi	Cat stance (literally "cat foot stance")		
Nidan	Literally translated as "second level." In the context of karate, nidan means second-degree black belt	**Tetsui-uchi**	Hammer-hand strike
		Tobi-geri	Jumping kick
Nihon	In karate competitions, this means "two points"	**Tode**	Okinawan unarmed fighting style, literally translated as "Chinese fist." The characters for tode are pronounced "karate" in Japanese
Nukite-uchi	Spear-hand strike		
Oi-zuki	Stepping punch (literally translated as a "chasing punch")		
Osae-uke	Pressing block	**Tokui**	Literally translated as "speciality." A tokui kata is a kata that you select to perform in a grading or competition and that you are expected to have a particular skill in performing
Pinan	Original Okinawan name for Heian, meaning "peace"		

Tsukami-uke	Grasping block	**WKF**	World Karate Federation. International governing body for karate recognized by the International Olympic Committee
Tsuki	Punch (literally translated as "thrust"). The tsu sound changes whenever it is after another word, so tsuki becomes zuki in oi-zuki, gyaku-zuki, and so on	**Yama-zuki**	Mountain punch, a U-shaped punching posture named after the similar-looking Japanese character for mountain
Uchi-otoshi	Falling strike	**Yame**	Stop
Uchi-uke	Inside block	**Yasume**	Rest
Ude-uke	Forearm block	**Yoi**	Ready
Uke	Usually interpreted as a block in karate, but literally translated it means "reception." Judo and jiu jitsu practitioners call the person who is thrown the uke, meaning "the receiver." Karate practitioners might refer to the defender as the ukete, "the receiving hand"	**Yoi-dachi**	Ready stance
		Yoko keage	Side rising kick
		Yoko kekomi	Side thrusting kick
		Yori ashi	Sliding foot movement where the front foot moves first
Uraken-uchi	Back-fist strike	**Zenkutsu-dachi**	Front stance
Ushiro-geri	Back kick		

193

INDEX

Page numbers with "g" are glossary terms.

Also Available

The Shotokan Karate Bible

ASHLEY P. MARTIN

The most widely practiced style of karate is Shotokan Karate. As well as outlining the history of this traditional martial art, *The Shotokan Karate Bible* combines authoritative text and clear instructions with hundreds of stunning color photographs, and includes:

- Fully illustrated, detailed syllabus from beginner to black belt

- Step-by-step program and instructions for the beginner

- Tips for grading examinations

- Advanced tips for the expert

With superb detail and clearly marked color sections, color-coded by belt for easy reference, this book is a must for anyone practicing Shotokan Karate up to black belt level, and is the perfect introduction to the karate art.

Available from all good book stores and online.